SECRETS
OF A
CEO COACH

SECRETS

OF A

CEO COACH

YOUR PERSONAL TRAINING GUIDE TO THINKING LIKE A LEADER AND ACTING LIKE A CEO

D. A. BENTON

McGraw-Hill

NEW YORK   SAN FRANCISCO   WASHINGTON, D.C.   AUCKLAND   BOGOTÁ
CARACAS   LISBON   LONDON   MADRID   MEXICO CITY   MILAN
MONTREAL   NEW DELHI   SAN JUAN   SINGAPORE
SYDNEY   TOKYO   TORONTO

Library of Congress Cataloging-in-Publication Data

Benton, D. A. (Debra A.)
    Secrets of a CEO coach : your personal training guide to thinking
like a leader and acting like a CEO / Debra Benton.
        p.   cm.
    Includes index.
    ISBN 0-07-007108-X
    1. Leadership. 2. Executive ability. 3. Chief executive officers—
Psychology. 4. Coaching (Athletics) I. Title.
    HD57.7.B467   1998
    658.4'092—dc21   98-51527
                                                                    CIP

McGraw-Hill
A Division of The McGraw-Hill Companies

    7 8 9 10   DSH/DSH   0 1 0 9 8 7 6

ISBN 0-07-136075-1
(paperback edition of ISBN 0-07-007108-X)

*The editing supervisor was Paul R. Sobel and the production supervisor was
Sherri Souffrance. It was set in New Times Roman by MM Design 2000, Inc.*

Printed and bound by Quebecor/Martinsberg.

McGraw-Hill books are available at special quality discounts to use as pre-
miums and sales promotions, or for use in corporate training programs. For
more information, please write to the Director of Special Sales, McGraw-
Hill, Professional Publishing, Two Penn Plaza, New York, NY 10121-2298.
Or contact your local bookstore.

This book is printed on recycled, acid-free paper
containing a minimum of 50% recycled, de-inked fiber

CONTENTS

ACKNOWLEDGMENTS

A lifetime of thanks goes to my parents, Fred and Teresa Benton, who always set an excellent example.

To my coach—and husband—Rodney Sweeney.

My agent Michael Cohn, editor Mary Glenn, and associate Amy Williams.

And some special people in my life: Mindy Credi, Carol Ballock, Michelle Monfor Fitzhenry, Dr. Kelly Kesler, Ernest Howell, Nancy Albertini, Delores Doyle, Violetta Kapsalis Buhler, and Pam Manfredo Curtis.

Benton Management Resources, Inc., 2221 West Lake Street, Fort Collins, Colorado 80521.

SECRETS

OF A

CEO COACH

WHAT IS BUSINESS COACHING?

The personal coach . . . if high achievers like Tiger Woods and Donald Trump have one (or more) for their jobs, why shouldn't you have one for yours? A coach isn't a friend, a boss, an in-law, a professional acquaintance, or even a mentor. A coach is a person who gives private, one-on-one instruction to prepare a person for specialized or important work. The coaching need—in corporate life—may be in leadership development, speech delivery, business etiquette, personality enhancement, confidence building, communication skills, people skills, personal and public relations, managing upwards, managing difficult people, or even appearance.

There are coaches who specialize in crisis management. The CEO of Odwalla, the natural food company, hired a coach to help him deal with the press, the public, victims, and his own employees after tainted fruit juice allegedly killed a child and hospitalized six people across the country.

There are coaches who specialize in communication and presentation skills. Before the CEO of one cable company went to Wall Street to sell investors on his company's stock, he spent a day beforehand with a communications coach who worked with him on how to appear comfortable and competent when answering tough questions. The general manager of an Australian hotel had the opportunity to be interviewed for a job running one of Donald Trump's properties. The hotel manager used a coach to prepare himself. (Trump himself uses a coach to gain media exposure.) When John Elway taped television commercials for his numerous car dealerships, he employed an acting coach.

There are coaches who specialize in very specific circumstances. A medical doctor in Denver performs part-time as a professional expert witness in medical liability lawsuits. He retains a coaching specialist to prepare him for very particular courtroom rigors. A company that invented an ear implant device for the deaf needed FDA approval. Before he went to Washington, D.C., the CEO met several times with a coach to rehearse legislative presentations.

Although different coaches have different specialties and techniques, their common objective is to raise performance, in other words, to help you enhance the good qualities you have and help you acquire other important qualities you may be lacking.

It's a fact that people who excel often make use of private coaches in their careers. Another fact is that it's very expensive—from $2500 to $10,000 per program. But coaching shouldn't be available only to the rich and famous. While the average person can't afford to pay such fees, average people in many ways cannot afford to miss out on what a coach can do for them. This book changes that. It makes executive-level coaching available to everyone—people at every level who have the potential to excel. All they need is access to the right techniques, advice, and information.

I've been a personal coach for more than 20 years. In fact, four of the six cases just cited were clients I coached. I've coached executives in seventeen different countries and in companies such as Mattel, Gillette, Hewlett-Packard, Motorola, Nabisco, Pepsi, DuPont, United Airlines, Colgate, AT&T, Citibank, Unilever, FMC,

AlliedSignal, Fannie Mae, Sprint, and McKinsey & Company. I've coached mayoral and gubernatorial candidates and even one running for the U.S. presidency. I've seen what kind of potential can develop when good advice is given to people.

In this book I provide you with the "inside info" on those expensive coaching sessions. You'll learn the questions you need to ask yourself in preparation, the tools to fit the job at hand, the variety of

Jack and I were to spend the day together in a coaching session. His employer, Sprint, had sent him to meet with me. A senior executive at the company had been coached by me a few years prior and felt Jack was ready for some similar advice. We started promptly at 9:00 a.m.

At 10:30 a.m. my secretary interrupted us to say Jack's secretary was on the telephone and needed to talk with him immediately. Naturally we took a break.

A few minutes later he returned with an odd grin on his face. I asked if everything was all right at the office. He explained, "I wasn't too enthused about this meeting. I thought it might be some touchy-feely-pseudopsychological stuff. So I arranged with my secretary to call me at exactly 10:30 this morning. I figured by then I could tell if it was worth my time. If it wasn't, I would tell you that an emergency came up and I had to return to my office."

"So what did you tell her?" I asked.

"I told her she didn't need to call me again. I can tell already this is definitely worth my time!"

You too might feel skeptical at the thought of being sent to a business coaching session. But as Jack quickly found out, you shouldn't. A coaching session is really a fantastic opportunity.

targets possible, the strategies to go forward, and the fallback plans you can rely on to help in a pinch. My techniques will give you confidence, and allow you to be able to go out and compete with the heavy hitters on an equal playing field.

In this book I'm your co-coach. If you utilize my advice I can guarantee that your performance and that of the organization you represent will increase. If it doesn't, I'll personally give you the money back on this book.

COACHES ARE NEEDED MORE THAN EVER

In today's competitive business environment a business coach isn't a luxury. It's a necessity. In a radically changing world new work habits are required. Even if you have a good reputation today, that does not guarantee continued success tomorrow. You need to constantly condition, motivate, and refresh your work style and behavior.

More information has been delivered in the last 30 years than during the previous 500. A single weekday copy of *The New York Times* today dispenses more information than the average person had access to in a *lifetime* a few hundred years ago. Companies spend more money on computing and communications than on industrial, mining, farm, and construction equipment combined. "Knowledge" is becoming more important than "product."

You're swamped keeping up with the demands of doing your job. Your formal schooling is long since completed. You don't have the time to attend a workshop or seminar every week. So how do you learn the necessary new things? From a personal coach. The bottom line is: If others are thinking about coaching and you aren't, you're at a competitive disadvantage. So you have to *become your own coach*. With the right instruction it can be done.

WHAT DOES A PERSONAL COACH DO AND WHY IS IT IMPORTANT?

I get a lot of questions about how coaching works. Here are a few of them:

What exactly does a personal business coach do?

A coach works with you privately to provide objective, professional direction to increase your performance by helping you enhance what you have and acquire what you need. Frequently, a coaching session is prompted by a career turning point that requires specialized advice. A turning point can be a new promotion; being passed over for a promotion; a move into a new job or industry; a change in reporting, job requirements, or responsibilities; or perhaps a new boss.

Why is there a need today more than ever?

To survive and thrive in today's competitive environment, it's not just *what* you know. Of course, you need to be extremely competent, but you also must stand out from the crowd in the "soft" side of business—be memorable, impressive, credible, genuine, trusted, and liked. As one of my clients once said, "My role in the company is very visible but they fail to see me." That's a perfect example of why coaching is needed today more than ever.

Why is personal coaching such a hot subject in corporate circles and such a growing business?

Careerwise, ambitious people want to avail themselves of anything that will help them grow and improve. Some choose face-lifts. Some choose "style" lifts. A coach works on the latter. *Good* managers want to help their people do better. Typically more objective than the individual employee, the boss can point out developmental needs. That's what the proliferation of performance appraisals is all about. Once needs are pointed out, some companies choose to follow up by providing an expert who can help the employee acquire the necessary traits. Most commonly this occurs when an individual is promoted from a "doer" job to a "manager/leader" job.

"Companies will promote someone before they give them a lick of training about how to stay out of trouble," says Joseph Straub, a former Burlington Industries manager. "There's an automatic expectation that you know what to do," says Sari Factor, Vice President of McDougal Littell. It's a fact: People often don't know what to do, and they sure aren't going to admit it!

Coaching is a growing business because companies have experienced the success of sending an employee to a good teacher to fix a specialized area. It's a lot cheaper for the company to "help fix" a current employee than to fire the person, risking a lawsuit, finding an interim replacement, recruiting the new person (generally at a cost of 33 percent of their salary), and then going through the orientation period, which is typically a less productive time. The bottom line is that coaching saves the company money.

When in a person's career is coaching needed?

The best time to get maximum receptivity to coaching advice is after some *setback* or a *leapfrog* event. The setback could be something like missing out on a promotion, losing an account, or suffering a decline of confidence due to something on the job. The leapfrog event could be receiving a promotion, gaining a new (significant) account, or wanting to improve confidence and competence—to leapfrog ahead of the competition. It could be as simple as turning forty, or fifty, a divorce, a death in the family, any eye-opening event that causes you to reevaluate, reflect, and decide to recharge your career.

Another particularly good time is *any time* you want to cease relying on your sheer brilliance and start availing yourself of all the other ways you can influence upwards, persuade and affect colleagues, sell your ideas, put your mark on a project, stand out from the crowd, and fit in with the powers that be—all that intangible stuff!

Let's take a break for some self-examination.

- Do I manage my boss well? Do I know how to?
- Am I able to successfully sell my ideas?
- Do I get the credit my work is due? If not, can I change that?
- Do I achieve results but in an unpleasant way?
- Do I have the "people skills" necessary to lead, not just boss people?
- Do people like me at work?
- Do I like my work?
- Do I stand out in any way, or do I just blend in with the crowd?
- Do I step up to the bat and take control of the power that can be mine?
- Do people treat me the way I think they should?
- Do I speak up and assert myself in meetings so people know my contributions?
- Can I make my position clear?
- Do I know how to "toot my own horn?" Do I know when I should?
- Can I change these things and still be myself? (Let me take the liberty to answer this one for you: "Yes, definitely yes.")

Who makes a good coach?

A good coach is someone qualified, objective, and skilled at motivating behavioral change. It's a person who can establish rapport with a wide range of people, ask the right questions, assess problem behaviors, and keep track of effective and not-so-effective behaviors. It's important that the individual suspend judgment and be a helpful colleague, not a competitor.

Another important coaching skill is an understanding of how to criticize constructively, be sensitive when pointing out problems, provide positive encouragement, and care for the self-esteem of the "coachee." The end result of good coaching is improved business performance for the individual and saving a valuable resource for the company.

I've just explained what makes a good coach. Since this book is to help you coach yourself, ask yourself:

- Can I be objective about myself?
- Am I motivated to change?
- Do I really want to deal effectively with a wide range of people?
- Am I willing to ask myself (and others) tough questions about myself?
- Will I honestly and thoroughly assess my problem areas?
- Will I keep track of my change and progress?
- Will I try to help others in their self-development?
- Am I worth all the effort? (Let me again, take the liberty to answer this one for you, "Yes, definitely yes."

What happens in a coaching session?

You start by reviewing your personal and professional background, how you got to where you are, where you are in your career, why you want coaching, what you hope to gain from the session, and where you want to go in your life. You complete self-assessment materials along with your manager(s), peer(s), and subordinate(s). The 360-degree evaluation establishes the baseline to work from. Several hours of discussion provide a professional assessment from the coach, and specific feedback is provided to meet the targets agreed upon. Advice may revolve around anything from appearance to decision-making ability to conflict management. It will almost certainly include attitude management, physical comportment, and interpersonal communication. In this book these three are called mental energy, physical energy, and emotional energy.

The coach and the person being coached agree on an agenda and timetable. An effective coach not only gives good advice but offers that advice in a manner recipients can internalize and make their own, so they can still feel true to themselves. It's important to feel you can still be yourself, or you'll never be comfortable with the new, improved version. A day-long session wraps up with a "trigger list" of actions and activities to implement *the next day,* week, and month(s). That session is followed up with a debriefing for the coachee's manager, along with a written action plan from the client. That plan makes sure the coach and the person being coached are always speaking the same language. Every two weeks, the client and coach talk to update each other, restrategize, and report on progress. Six months later, a subsequent session repeats the process and prepares the client for the new levels of challenges and opportunities.

Here are some examples of entries from the trigger lists of some pretty high-powered business leaders. Even if you aren't a CEO (yet), take a look at these and see which ones would be useful for your own situation.

- *Improve my personal and professional presence.* Be aware of my physical bearing, posture, and comportment. Do what it takes mentally, physically, and emotionally to communicate self-confidence, not self-consciousness?

- *Deal effectively with difficult people.* Control my attitudes and perspective on things. Don't let others control my perspective. And don't be lazy or forget to manage my attitudes, either.

- *Work with people who aren't that smart.* Be more generous towards others' actions; be less judgmental. Think, "If I were in their shoes, I might act the exact same way."

- *Handle business social gatherings well.* Take charge and initiate conversations with strangers before I'm invited to, before the the ice is broken, or before I feel comfortable. Just do it, forget my discomfort, and focus on learning what I can at this gathering and making others feel comfortable.

- *Be more personable versus just seeking results at any cost.* Ask others about themselves, their interests, successes, setbacks, dreams. Listen well and learn from their experiences. Share my own as well so we develop an affinity and rapport through the discovery of "common ground."

- *Stay "on" even when I don't feel it.* Stop frowning when listening to others (it makes me appear suspicious or at least scared). Maintain an affable expression even when I don't feel it.

- *Communicate effectively but interestingly.* Insert good humor into serious conversations to improve communication, develop rapport, reduce others' tension, and relax my own stressful feelings. Tell useful stories, anecdotes, and illustrations to make sure my communication is clear and interesting.

- *Lead; don't just manage or boss people.* Do all I can to maintain the self-esteem of people around me. Ask opinions of others so they feel valued and needed.

How will you benefit from coaching?

One of the best ways to answer this question is to share the remarks of people who have actually experienced a coaching situation.

- "The guidance on delivering a speech, organizing my thoughts, relating to the audience, and handling questions helped improve how I present myself and most important strengthened my self-confidence. As a result, I obtained the promotion I was seeking and am being considered for a new assignment."

- "I have a new faith in 'Guardian Angels.' I feel like I have one watching over my personal improvement efforts as I try to manage my relationships with people up, down, and alongside me, rather than letting them just happen."

- "In the time it takes to fly from Los Angeles to New York [the approximate length of a coaching session], I received enough business acumen on selling my ideas to last a lifetime. Now I always ask questions to see what my clients want to achieve, maintain, and avoid; questions about how decisions are made and how they plan to pay for it. Then I give them what they asked for, since I know it clearer than anyone else."

- "Coaching saved my professional life by making me aware of the power I have to influence people if I'll just slow down, think things through, and act accordingly."

- "I walked out of the session and closed a $15 million contract based on the strategy we laid out for presenting my position, supporting it with good stories, asking questions to learn about objections, and suggesting alternatives that met their and my goals."

- "I wish I had known this stuff 10 years ago—about walking into a room and making an immediate impact from the handshake on. I thought if I produced results, that was all that was necessary. Now I've learned that at the CEO level, style is instrumental in achieving those results."

Needless to say, you will benefit in increased awareness, confidence, and the ability to act in a more effective manner with people up and down the ladder, inside and outside the organization. When you raise your personal performance and therefore the performance of your organization, you also create job security.

How do companies benefit?

- They save a valuable resource because employees don't quit for lack of support and move to another company that cares more about them.

- They save money because they don't have to pay to recruit a replacement for someone who quit, or replace a person they had to fire because she or he lacked the necessary "soft" side of business leadership.

- They improve morale because good people feel valued when the company "invests" in them.

- They become more competitive and unique because they have a motivated, happy, skilled team who can handle most any situation they are faced with in an effective manner, both in substance and style.

As Dave Powelson, the President of TRI-R Systems said, "Everyone in my company needs this, it's like breakfast."

Can individuals coach themselves?
Yes. Definitely. People do it all the time. Of course, it is easier and more rewarding if you eliminate the guessing, trial and error, and misdirection and substitute *proven* techniques and approaches. That's the rationale behind this book. It condenses 25 years of on-the-job information. Whether professionally coached or self-coached, *results occur only if you take the necessary action.* No matter how good a coach is, if you don't *want* to change, then nothing will.

CASES FOR COACHES
Following are eight case studies of actual coaching situations. Each is broken down by situation, the coaching approach devised for that situation, and the results obtained. These cases help illustrate typical problems and solutions from coaching sessions, and they are intended to motivate you, to help generate ideas, and to provide support.

CASE # 1

SITUATION   An up-and-coming manager had moved quite rapidly up the corporate ranks. He was creative, resourceful, driven, and fairly self-confident. The confidence turned to slight arrogance. As he started working with the CEO of the company, who was used to calling the shots, egos clashed. The company faced losing a great performer, because the CEO certainly wasn't going to leave—or change.

APPROACH   The first two hours of the coaching session were spent working on attitude alone—toward himself and others, especially others in positions of power. This entailed paying particularly close attention to *how* the young man said what he said, his verbal and nonverbal explanations about situations. It also involved pointing out, in a kind but straightforward manner, some of the overdone bravado he displayed and how he could change his dealings with the CEO by changing that manner. Specifically, he learned how to remain secure in himself while staying appreciative of the ego and self-esteem of the guy at the top. If he'd slow down, i.e., think before he spoke, and put himself in the position of the CEO, he'd get along better with him, be more highly valued by the CEO, and maybe become one himself.

(continued)

He needed to show that he consistently helps and guides people, instead of developing a reputation for strewing bodies, his boss, the CEO, included, all over the playing field in his ambitious climb upward. When made aware of how his attitudes toward others showed, he decided to change them in order to meet his objective more "acceptably." Nothing else needed changing.

RESULT   The person in this instance stayed with the company despite offers to go elsewhere. The day of coaching "turned his life around and had the most impact of any help he ever received because someone candidly but pleasantly 'called' his behavior and gave him something constructive to do about things." The CEO considered the change overwhelming too, "He knows how to pull out the right gun when he needs it now."

CASE #2

SITUATION Employees were rampantly resigning from a company because they didn't like dealing with an in-
timidating 6'6", 240-pound supervisor.

APPROACH Despite his size, in truth, this guy was very shy, a
little timid, and didn't easily warm up to, or in turn,
get people to warm up to him. Over time, his actual dealings with people were fine. Initially,
though, he was scaring people with his bull in the
bush manner. What was needed was to turn his
"huge physical being" into an "immense positive
presence." In other words, give others someone to
look up to versus be afraid of.

First, he practiced standing with good posture,
head and spine straight, chest lifted off his pelvis,
shoulders back, like a member of a *winning* football team instead of a *losing* one, so to speak. Then
he practiced literally walking into a board room,
meeting room, or wherever and pausing for a split
second to announce "I'm here" in an approachable,
affable manner. The split-second pause prevented
him from rushing into someone else's turf, allowing
them to acknowledge him on their own terms. It also
gave him a chance for a slow, deep breath before
he opened his mouth so his words came out clearly.

Again, with good posture, he practiced walking
purposefully toward a person he was meeting,

(continued)

pause a split second, then reach and give a firm handshake palm to palm (whether it was a man or a woman). He worked on giving three pumps rather than one or two, and then on purposefully retrieving his hand instead of flopping it down to his side. The point was to communicate that the handshake *meant* something and to set a productive, constructive tone to the meeting.

He then practiced sitting down with good posture, positioning his arms in an asymmetrical manner (one arm on an armrest, one not, for example) to appear relaxed, and more important, to relax others! Finally, he cultivated an at-ease facial expression that said, "I'm listening to *you* because what you have to say is very important, and likewise, I want you to feel comfortable, competent, and confident to do business together."

By changing this first *physical* impression and maintaining the new presence when walking down the hallway, receiving a guest in his office, giving a speech, or working the room at an office social gathering, he reduced his own tension and made others feel at ease around him and proud to be associated with him.

RESULTS

He said, "Most people like me once they get to know me. The problem was they never got to know me. I'm very grateful that's changed." By the way, now he's described as "impressive" by his co-workers.

CASE #3

SITUATION   A female director, who reported to the senior vice-president, knew more about the companywide work than anyone in the organization. But she was reticent to speak up. She didn't want to interrupt or just "hear herself talk" as she saw others do. She was not certain her point would really add significant value to the conversation, so she frequently said nothing. Plus, she almost "froze up" when talking to people in rooms with "heavy, dark furniture," as she described the executive offices.

APPROACH   This person kept a log from meetings she had attended over the last month. She and her coach went through each entry one by one and structured what contribution or assertion she could have (and should have) volunteered in a clear, succinct, confident manner.

For the next month of meetings, she agreed to make some "contribution" or "insertion of herself" every 15 minutes. That meant only four times in a one-hour meeting. (That's not too much to ask of yourself either!) She could "contribute" a point, compliment someone else's point, ask that a comment to be repeated, affirm someone else's comment, thank someone for their contribution, or give a deep, purposeful nod while someone else was talking and simply say "yes" in agreement.

(continued)

To prepare for future meetings the same three-step structure was followed: (1) think through what is likely to happen, (2) consider how you are likely to respond, and (3) plan a couple of alternative actions or responses that are different from others and different from what she'd typically do.

She also learned how to get others to contribute more and take pressure off herself by the judicious use of probing questions—asked three times to really get to the truth. (Asking only once often gets superficial responses.)

RESULT This employee's boss, the Senior VP, remarked later that he would have paid "four times what he did [for the coaching] because of the changes he saw." And the director refers to her newly acquired tools as, "a new toy box of skills to use." She's now listened to and heard as much as she deserves.

CASE #4

SITUATION   A man with superb knowledge of his firm and the industry he worked in was expecting to become CEO. He was devastated when an outsider was named chief.

APPROACH   After some discussion, this executive concluded that he had relied too much on his intellectual ability and competence without cultivating the leadership and emotional maturity required in business. He needed a pick-me-up of new ideas to prove to himself and the powers-that-be his readiness for a CEO job. They saw him as a good manager and doer, not a leader.

He set out and followed a *daily* detail-oriented, planned routine based on being aware of his style:

1. To continuously improve in a new area.

2. To increase originality by doing what others don't think of or have the courage to do.

3. To risk being a little gutsy and a tad theatrical while still being good at his job intellectually.

4. To do all he could to maintain the self-esteem of people around him.

5. To think, act, talk, relate, and *look* like a leader.

(continued)

In other words, he fully embraced the mental, physical, and emotional energy required as a person moves up the ladder. Thinking that being result's oriented and deadline driven is sufficient is naive. This executive, and you, must be all of that *PLUS* having an awareness of your effect on others and the ability to control it.

RESULT The executive in this case eventually left the company for another CEO position and is now viewed as the best in his field. He was recently featured in *Forbes* magazine. He summed up the problem this way, "At some level I was aware of what I should do in dealing with people, but I took it lightly. Now I pay more attention."

So you can take heart in the fact everyone who goes anywhere in this life has coaching. You are not alone in your need. You are smart because you are working on this now!

21

CASE #5

SITUATION   A newly promoted executive, although very competent, had several nervous habits. As an example, his boss pointed out, "He doesn't have an executive laugh."

APPROACH   Here, a seemingly insignificant natural habit was hindering the exec's progress. His case did not so much involve adding skills as persistently eliminating self-defeating behaviors. Simply by removing self-imposed hurdles he found he could have authority but still be himself.

Engaged in conversation on a number of subjects, after a point, the executive forgot he was being taped and let down his guard. Regarding his hair, he said it was once so long it got him fired from a job, but now he sports an "eight-inch part" (bald!). He talked about his favorite vacations with his wife and how on their first trip together they both got food poisoning and spent six days being sick together in their hotel room. There were moments of career pride in which he was called on by his state senator to do the introduction at a national meeting. The point of all this was to capture his style on tape. When he listened to the tape, he admitted, "I sure sound silly and nervous. That's awful." First came awareness. Then came the self-discipline to slow down and monitor the volume,

(continued)

range, and speed of his laugh. He was instructed by his coach to leave voice-mail messages over the next few weeks, relating some anecdote so the coach could hear his progress. On one follow-up message he commented that he practices his new laugh with friends and family and even they notice a difference, and he added, "Things must be going well at work."

RESULT   Everyone around this fellow—his co-workers, boss, even his wife—feel relief and gratefulness that he was coached to become self-aware without becoming self-conscious. He now sounds like the memorable, impressive, genuine, trustworthy, likable person he is.

CASE #6

SITUATION   A Chinese woman from a division office in Shanghai was transferred to headquarters in Chicago.
Although she spoke and dressed "American," her
personality and training was all Chinese. Males
and females many levels below her were running
roughshod over her authority.

APPROACH   A trigger list of encounters she experienced was
compiled and analyzed point by point and a situation management plan was created for each. Naturally, it was up to her to methodically carry it out.

A history review revealed everything from her
traditional Chinese upbringing and culture to the
nontraditional job she was currently doing, nontraditional, that is, for a Chinese person, especially
a female. She and her coach looked for ways she
could be true to "her roots" but also assimilate
into the global marketplace in which she lived and
worked. They also addressed ways to reconcile
traditional "gender roles" and getting things done
"like a man."

When the results of her 360 degree interviews
were analyzed, she was pleasantly surprised at
how many people valued her abilities, far beyond
how she valued herself. She finally accepted the
fact she was "adequate" to do the job at hand.

(continued)

24

To complete the strategy, she was coached on how to remain positive and enthusiastic while dealing with difficult people or circumstances unfamiliar to her. She came to accept that although all of us like to be liked, realistically, we will all have "foes." With this new understanding, she now sees how foes, jerks, and enemies help her be better. She's even learned to be thankful for them, as you will see in Chapter 6.

RESULT

Both the woman in this case and her boss called her time in coaching "the best training experience she ever had." She got promoted back to Shanghai, but stays in touch periodically, frequently sending traditional Chinese presents. She now plans to start her own international trading firm.

CASE #7

SITUATION   The president of a small Midwestern electrical supply company was immensely popular among his peers. Active in his industry association, he found himself elected president. Overnight, he turned from being a small fish in a small pond to becoming a big fish in a humongous pond.

APPROACH   This guy knew the industry backwards and forwards. But what he needed to know was how to better deal with public presentations (and public criticism), political presence, and other performance roles required in this highly visible position. Showmanship, confidence, and delivery under pressure, anywhere, anytime became the focus of his coaching. That effort also concentrated on increasing his inquisitiveness, his flexibility, his ability to discuss serious issues with a wide range of people, and on making his storytelling to be more interesting and entertaining.

He updated his hairstyle and wardrobe so that his basic appearance was "with the times."

He made a point to literally and figuratively "pat people on the back" every day. He tried to do all he could to maintain the self-esteem of people around him.

Using his "platform," he boldly initiated contact with people he would never have dreamed of

(continued)

calling before. Every day he added a new contact to his "cadre" list. When the association he headed made news, he simply made sure that everyone on the list received a copy.

He became known for his creativity and resourcefulness in solving problems because he practiced the simple principle of "doing the opposite" of what most people do, which you will learn about in Chapter 4.

RESULT　He so enjoyed the power of the association presidency that after his year was up, he decided to have his wife run the electrical business and he became a lobbyist in Washington, D.C.

CASE #8

SITUATION A lot of men and women of all backgrounds who seek coaching help are often described with some variation of "off-the-charts bright but doesn't step up to bat and take control of the power that can be theirs." When they walk into a room, there is little or no impact. They're too often the "who" in the question, "who's that?"

APPROACH In every situation you start by accepting the fact that you can, want to, and need to make changes. Change is inevitable as one moves up any mountain. Change starts with an objective "sizing yourself up" incorporating with opinions of others. From that soul-searching comes a "trigger list" of problem areas to attack.

Each problematic area is attacked with a view toward the mental, physical, and emotional energy required. For example, changes in:

- The self-talk you give yourself
- The way you think about others
- The fact you have to catch and correct your thinking 100 times a day
- The skill of thinking of the opposite when the standard isn't working
- The self-discipline to create new patterns and habits

(continued)

- The willingness to slow down and think things through instead of relying on old habits
- The actions that create the first and the lasting impression you *want* to create
- The physical control you need to exert in your posture, walk, smile
- The basic appearances that make you memorable, impressive, credible, genuine, and trusted
- The way you sound and what you say when you open your mouth
- The tenacity to do all you can to maintain the self-esteem of people around you
- The way you think about the "jerks" in your life and the fact that they can be your best coaches
- The "book value" increase to your company, but more important, to yourself and your family
- The humor you're willing to interject into serious conversations so you relax yourself and reduce other people's tension, while improving communication
- The affable nature you take on, even when you don't feel it
- The bold actions you will take to get the job done regardless of your personal insecurities, fears, or hesitations.

RESULT   Almost everyone who fits the description above is willing to make the jump into a "makeover" of image and organizational impact and to develop a

(continued)

29

style that reflects substance, versus one that *undermines* their substance.

You, too, can be one of those who "gets it" in life. With a knowledge of the "secrets" of coaching you'll get it sooner than others and it will last longer than others because of your own effort and determination.

Do you notice a common theme in these cases? All of the approaches are things you can do yourself. The purpose of this book is to give you lots of options you probably never thought of or hadn't given yourself permission to exercise. Your job is to capitalize on them. The payoff? Your work performance will increase (you'll probably make more money), and you'll be more focused and confident, as if you've met with a coach in person. This is a guarantee.

DO THIS FOR YOURSELF AND THE IMPORTANT PEOPLE IN YOUR LIFE

Here's a true story that started 16 years ago. A company president who had read about my consulting work contacted me to work with his son. The son was getting out of military service and was soon to take over his father's company. The father wanted me to coach him in the areas of people skills and presence so he could lead the business more effectively. The son had grown up around the company so he knew the "substance" side of the operation, but he didn't know the "style" side.

The father described his son like this, "He's a good guy, but he's kind of strange. He has these weird facial expressions, he doesn't deal well with people, and frankly, they don't like him. But he is my son and I want him to take over my business." I talked with the son to see how we'd work together on the various development issues. He was not convinced of the necessity and made the choice to not work with anyone, including me, on things that didn't seem that important. Coincidentally, around this time I met the son's wife and newborn baby boy while walking in the park one day.

A couple of months ago, sixteen years after that conversation, I received a telephone call from the son, who had long since taken over his father's company. "Are you still doing the kind of coaching where you help people be more effective?" he asked.

I said, "Yes."

"Do you ever work with teenagers? I have a 16-year-old son who is a good kid but he's kind of strange. He has these weird facial expressions, he doesn't deal well with people, and he's not very likable. Do you think you could help him?"

Very interesting. The point: Whatever you do well (or poorly) tends to pass on to people around you. There are a million reasons to start coaching yourself today. There's only one that truly matters, the people that mean the most to you.

MISSTEPS COST BIG-TIME (and Usually Big Money)

Frankly, fewer missteps are allowed today. One of the top key executives to Tony O'Reilly, CEO of Heinz, and I were talking about missteps in business. I asked, "How do you handle mistakes?" He answered, "I correct them before I make them." The world rewards those who catch on to what's happening. What's happening in the upper levels of business today is the use of a partner (a coach) in a career. In this case, that partner has to be *you*. You can expect your employer to expect more of you. As the Putnam Investments advertisement reads, "You think you understand the situation, but what you don't understand is that the situation just changed." When you coach yourself, you prepare yourself for that inevitable situation.

The goal of a personal coach is to help you *be more,* to bring out your best potential, guide you to better deal with the future, and make you a more valuable employee. A coach also assists you in changing behaviors that can threaten or derail a career. Winging it won't cut it. Resistance to change is a career killer or at best a dead-end street. This book is about being smart and changing early to satisfy the people who pay for your work.

A college grad can leapfrog ahead of peers with good coaching—self-administered. A seasoned middle manager can discover that *it's never too late* to recharge one's career with good coaching—self-administered.

Everybody needs coaching. *And* everyone who is successful uses one. They just don't tell you!

Fact is, even the strongest performers need assistance to grow and compete. The CEO of Fruit of the Loom, Bill Farley, says that the amount of valuable information you get from personal coaching "is like drinking from a fire hydrant." If you want to have so much value to your organization that something very important would be missing if you left, *get cracking today.* Because you're on your way to being a coach to the most important client in the world—yourself!

YOU KNOW YOU'RE READY FOR COACHING WHEN . . .

You work incredibly hard and you are an outstanding performer at your job. You were taught that if you worked hard, had experience and education, were smart, computer literate, motivated, modest, and honest, good things would happen and you'd get ahead in this world. You'd make a decent income, enjoy a reasonable retirement, and you'd pave the way for your kids to do even more than you. But it's not exactly turning out that way. It's not disastrous, but it is a little frustrating and irritating. Even when your work satisfies you, it doesn't seem to always satisfy your boss. You find yourself considering changing fields and searching for different work. Too much time is spent squabbling with colleagues or hoping for a little positive reinforcement or recognition from management. And you are forever lobbying for a promotion that is past due. It seems there is some intangible skill missing that you can't quite put your finger on.

A McKinsey & Company partner put it this way, "In life there are people who are snowball makers and people who are snowball throwers. At the top, you have to be both." The first requirement of a successful career is getting prepared, getting qualified, and getting established in your field. The second requirement of a career is the "intangible" stuff written about in this book. The first requirement causes you to work hard; the second causes you to think hard. It's like golf: Skilled players don't just hit the ball straight and hard, they "think" their way around the golf course. To work up to your ability, stop working harder, and start thinking.

A *Fortune* 200 firm completed a very high-profile search for a woman to run a division of the company. Two months into her contract the company president said this about her, "We got the skill set and thinking we wanted. She has the intellectual capacity and more. She's strategic, effectively leads cross-functionally, understands concepts, and brings them forward. Overall, she's a collegial manager. The struggle we have is with her confidence, personality, and presence. Her communication skills and delivery of a message are uncomfortable. She's awkward and clunky visually. Verbally, she's apologetic and recessive in her manner. She seldom asks questions, and in her position, she should be asking questions all the time. If she doesn't change, people will wonder why she's here. Reality is, her colleagues aren't forgiving of her style."

She spent a day in coaching and went through everything you will learn in this book. It has been more than six months now. Daily, she uses discipline, courage, and technique in executing what she learned about herself and business at the top levels. Today, the company thinks they have a real "find." She's happy, was recently promoted, and makes more money than she ever thought possible. She lives in the house of her dreams and is setting an example for her children at home on how to have both substance *and* style.

You can run with it or get run over by it. *It* is the realization that how you do your job is as important as the job you do. The important business press recognizes that the CEO with the right stuff is increasingly seen as having superior general management and leadership abilities, not specialized industry knowledge. That trend is only likely to grow. "If you're not realistic about this, you're dead," says Sam Sanderson, CEO of Savvis Communications.

THE STYLE VERSUS SUBSTANCE ARGUMENT

What's more important, style or substance? The undeniable truth: Substance is necessary but not sufficient. All substance being equal, the tiebreaker is always style. And although that style frequently may be hard to quantify and define, it makes all the difference in the world. If you feel this is not fair or right, you have a point. But it is reality. You can be mad, fight it, and deny it all you want. You will lose the struggle. But let me be perfectly clear; I am not suggesting you *replace* style for substance. Just don't make the mistake of depending on substance alone.

Thomas Jefferson wrote, "In matters of style, swim with the current. In matters of principle, stand like a rock." Be strong but be smart. Bill Gates, CEO of Microsoft and one of the wealthiest people in the world, has been widely quoted as saying brains are all that matters because you can teach smart people anything they need to know. Brains are required, of course. But people with lots of brain cells frequently need to be taught to use their smarts to develop style.

"It's interesting that hard skills (statistical analysis, crunching numbers, devising grand corporate strategies) are considered better than soft," says C. Thomas Howard, professor of finance and director of MBA programs[1] at the University of Denver's Daniels College of Business. "But when people go into management, it's the soft skills that dominate almost everything they do. They are the ones that make the difference in career success."

The dean's executive advisory board of the University of Arkansas, which is made up of working presidents and senior executives of companies throughout the Southeast, was asked what they wanted to see most in an MBA graduate today. Their answer was, "Someone who is articulate, persuasive, and can read a balance sheet—in that order." The soft skills—being articulate, persuasive, and effective—are where most people need coaching. One MBA program director was quoted in *The Wall Street Journal* as saying, "If they [MBAs] can handle a stand-up comedy routine, they can handle anything."

This is an apt analogy. One of the ways I earned scholarship money during college was being in beauty pageants, most of which involve a "talent" portion as well as interview, appearance, etc. Singing and dancing were out for me, so I decided to try a stand-up comedy routine. For practice, I'd go to nightclubs that had entertainment, and when the band took a break, I'd go on stage and do my comedy routine. When I look back, I think either I was incredibly stupid *or* incredibly courageous. Many times I was "booed" big-time. Occasionally, an audience was generous. But I did learn *style* in delivery: timing, pacing, what works with an audience and what doesn't, and when to make an exit—the soft skills, all of which I use today as a professional speaker.

In Coopers & Lybrand's corporate brochure they describe their core values as integrity, teamwork, mutual respect, and personal responsibility, the style side of business, the softer side. The technical side of the world's largest accounting/consulting firm isn't emphasized. Granted, it's assumed. And the same is true for you. Once you reach management and executive levels, your substance is assumed. What your bosses want to see is if you fit in, reflect the corporate culture's image (as well as their's), and if you understand the "code." At the National Western Stock Dog Trials the winning trainer explained about his border collie: "The best dog has style in dealing with the sheep." Substance and style, they permeate in all walks of life!

Pepsi-Cola rates its top middle and senior management people on thought leadership, people leadership, organizational impact, and professional maturity. By the time individuals get to that level in the organization, their managers rightfully assume competence. What they are looking for is the *style*. If you don't have it, you are out, regardless of how brilliant you are.

Mortimer B. Zuckerman is the chairman of a new publication that Thomas R. Evans publishes. It's called *Fast Company*. In a recent article on leadership they did a piece on FedEx's system for rating leaders. Here in summary form are that system's nine elements:

1. *Charisma.* Instills faith, respect, and trust. Has a special gift of seeing what others need to consider. Conveys a strong sense of mission.

2. *Individual consideration.* Coaches, advises, and teaches people who need it. Actively listens and gives indications of listening. Gives newcomers a lot of help.

3. *Intellectual stimulation.* Gets others to use reasoning and evidence, rather than unsupported opinion. Enables others to think about old problems in new ways. Communicates in a way that forces others to rethink ideas that they had never questioned before.

4. *Courage.* Willing to stand up for ideas, even if they are unpopular. Does not give in to pressure or to others' opinions in order to avoid confrontation. Will do what's right for the company and for employees, even if it causes personal hardship.

5. *Dependability.* Follows through and keeps commitments. Takes responsibility for actions and accepts responsibility for mistakes. Works well independently of the boss.

6. *Flexibility.* Functions effectively in changing environments. When a lot of issues hit at once, handles more than one problem at a time. Changes course when the situation warrants it.

7. *Integrity.* Does what is morally and ethically right. Does not abuse management privileges. Is a consistent role model.

8. *Judgment.* Reaches sound and objective evaluations of alternative courses of action through logic, analysis, and comparison. Puts facts together rationally and realistically. Uses past experience and information to bring perspective to present decisions.

9. *Respect for others.* Honors and does not belittle the opinions or work of other people, regardless of their status or position.

Note how these leadership skills apply not only to ability but to style as well.

In the world of sports there are coaches who hit the right tone with their players, where there is a blend of motivation, toughness, organization, and leadership. Basketball coaches come to mind, like Rick Pitino of Boston, Pat Riley of Miami, and Phil Jackson of Chicago. They have what *USA Today* refers to as "juice." Coaches get juice through fair and honest treatment of people, gaining trust, learning from mistakes, understanding tactics, plus observation and patience in dealing with various situations. That's juice—the intangible, the soft, the style side. The person who thinks this can't be learned will probably remain in a subordinate or ineffective position. Getting it is completely doable. And it is completely crucial.

You can even take style to another level: *prana.* Prana is a Sanskrit word. It means "breath" or "life force." Your business qualifications combined with your prana makes for your all-important juice.

IT'S NEVER TOO LATE

Many of you don't have to worry about this right now, but most people find themselves middle-aged sooner than they'd care to have it happen. When it does happen, remember to take advantage of all the good things that come with age: varied experience, maturity and wisdom, perspective, confidence, relaxed attitudes, accumulated knowledge, decision-making ability, struggles that have been overcome, understanding people, past accomplishments, respect and distinction from peers, credibility, comfortable finances, professional contacts made, and the ability to empower others.

As long as you keep up with new technologies, avoid being pushed aside, employ up-to-date approaches, remain competitive and effective, stay healthy and have stamina, work well with young bosses and colleagues, deal with changing corporate cultures and values, maintain an energetic appearance, build financial security, and don't settle for mediocrity, you'll never get "old." It's like a friend, Mark Levine, who's a diamond broker. He was in Hong Kong on business and was meeting a client in the hotel lobby. He had described himself as, "six feet tall, brown hair, and mustache." But as Mark left his room, he glanced in the mirror and saw his hair and mustache were actually gray. They hadn't been brown in 20 years!

Recently, traveling on business, I walked past the mirror in my hotel room and for a second couldn't accept the reflection was me. I looked older than I felt. Thinking it was the poor lighting in the room, I called the front desk and requested brighter light bulbs. They didn't help. It was like one of those fun-house mirrors that makes you look bigger (and fatter) than you are. The moral of this story is that although it would be nice if mirrors reflected the full picture, including self image, they really just give back the externals.

We all grow older. Another friend, younger than I am, recently sent me a birthday card with this message: "No matter how old you get, I'll always be younger." Of course I *feel* young, but I have to remind myself that I'm no longer a young career person but a mature, *experienced* one dealing with younger people all around me.

Bob Greene, author of *The Fifty Year Dash,* says, "One of the absolute truths about being 50 at work is that never again can you be thought of as an up-and-comer. Not in any way. Not in any profession or field of endeavor. . . . You can be good at what you do; you can be successful. But a door has closed. You can't be a hotshot." Regardless of how close or far you are from 50, you can't turn back the clock. This instant is the right time to become more successful, *regardless of your age.* Anyone at any stage of life can do that. Older people have the same options as younger people. It's just that the time is compressed for them.

WHAT HOLDS YOU BACK?

Fear

First is fear. You know fear, that stuff that makes your stomach turn upside down, gives you butterflies, makes your palms sweat and underarms drip, causes your knees to knock and then buckle, and shoots beads of sweat that run down your back. Whoa! Calm down. Be cool. The greatest self-defeating behavior out there is consternation about everything, in other words, *fear*. You know fear: *F*alse *E*vidence that *A*ppears *R*eal.

Fears gets transferred into concerns about:

- Looking foolish
- Making mistakes
- Seeking approval
- _____ (Add your personal favorite to the list.)

You probably feel you never have enough time. Well, one of the biggest time wasters[2] in life is fear, because it causes hesitancy and procrastination. Save time. Be fearless. It gives you such flourish and panache! Get comfortable being a little on the edge every day. Get some moxie. Put yourself into a vulnerable position. Remember the pageants? Fear is walking across a fully lit stage, wearing high heels and a swimsuit, and pirouetting in front of thousands of people while trying to look comfortable and confident. To this day, I sometimes flash back to that stage before I walk into some big shot's office. At times, I even replay the theme song in my head as a mnenonic device to get me to embrace my fears and act comfortable, "There she is . . ." My company wouldn't exist if I didn't have the ability to look comfortable, cool, and collected when I'm actually not!

The only trepidation you should have is the fear of:

- Not being the best version of yourself
- Being left behind
- Being left without

In twenty-something years on the corporate playing field, I've seen my share of fear. But if you'll notice, other people are just as anxious, even important, titled, moneyed, scholarly people! Acting just a little less timid and a little more courageous than the other person makes you more memorable, impressive, credible, genuine, trusted, and liked. (This technique is discussed in more depth in Chapters 4, 5, and 6.) There is an old Chinese saying: Better to live one day as a lion than a dozen years as a sheep. It's one thing to have fear; it's another to have fear but not act. For the most part, you'll never get hurt as badly as you fear you'll get hurt. This life of yours is the only opportunity you'll ever get to show what you can do. *Let's go for it!* You can do anything, be anything, *if* you're willing to accept what comes along with it, that is, a little scariness. By the way, you'll also find that if you don't acknowledge trepidation, there is no trepidation at all.

Bob Mattick, coach of the Toronto Blue Jays, says, "A human being doesn't know how far he can go until he's pushed himself to the limit." Push yourself through those periods of hesitation, consternation, apprehension, and pure panic. As you get older, I'll guarantee you, you'll regret when you've been cowardly, *not* when you've been gutsy. Regardless of your age, you'll save a lot of time by choosing to *not* worry about what other people think about you.

Deepak Chopra said, "My biggest fear all my life was the fear of lack of approval. That was my driving force. But I'm in the process of relinquishing that fear." That's good for him to do, and for you! It cannot be put clearer than President Roosevelt's famous line, "We have nothing to fear but fear itself." If you want to improve, and improving is what coaching is all about, start with ceasing fear.

It's like when Ted Turner read the *Forbes* list of the 400 wealthiest people in the country and said, "We're a nation of lists. People like to move up on lists. The first time I looked at it and saw my name, I thought, 'Hmmmm, *I can do a little better.*'" To successfully coach yourself, you're going to have to do *a little better* in a number of behaviors, the least of which is being more gutsy and less fearful.

Australian aboriginals don't have birthday celebrations. To them a birthday means only getting older, not better. Instead, they celebrate getting better and wiser. That marks growth (and therefore aging) to them. How old would you be if your age was marked in growth? I promise that doing a little better will give you a great throbbing-temple-passion-pursuing feeling, and what a feeling it is, that defining moment of fearlessly handling something well. Ralph Waldo Emerson wrote, "Every day do one thing that makes you afraid." Anais Nin wrote, "I postpone death by living, by suffering, by error, by risking, by giving, by losing." and "Your life shrinks or expands in direct proportion to your amount of courage." Poet Rainer Maria Rilke said, "The purpose in life is to be defeated by greater and greater things." Only a bold approach can make a big difference quickly.

Fact is: If you have courage, and therefore are willing to risk, life can be very exciting. You can't wait for challenges to come to you, you have to go after them. That takes *mut* (the German word for courage). Growth comes from going beyond your comfort zone. That builds confidence. It does not mean rock climbing or doing a stand-up comedy routine, but as they put it at Coopers & Lybrand, BHAG (Big, Hairy, Audacious, Goals). BHAG is necessary if you want juice.

Technique

Aside from fear, the second self-defeating action is not spending the time required to figure out what to do differently. The motivation is there. The direction is there. But the exact steps to take today, tomorrow, and the next day—when yesterday's steps didn't work— are what's perplexing. That's what makes a good coach: a creative, resourceful information sharer—*valuable* information for career satisfaction and success, not the information hoarder so often found among co-workers.

If you know *what* to act on, you'll likely do it. If you could spend all day thinking about what to act on, you'd come up with some creative, resourceful ideas. BUT you have to spend your day doing your job. As your co-coach, my job *is* to spend all day thinking of fresh ways to handle old (and new) situations. My work is to stimulate your imagination to plausible, conceivable, reasonable, but nontypical approaches to everyday problems. As Robert Half put it, "When one teaches, two learns." No one has the right answers to all situations, because in reality there is no *right*. Perfection really isn't possible in this world. The answers just have to be better and different from what's come before.

Take the example of a young woman who is on track for making vice president in the professional firm where she works. One weekend, her boyfriend, who lives in a different city, proposed marriage. She received a gorgeous engagement ring, which she naturally wanted to wear. But wearing it would get the partners in the firm (all male) prematurely curious and even concerned about her loyalty and longevity with the firm. Sexism still lives in corporate America. The question of a male getting engaged seldom gets followed with, "But will he stay with the firm?" Assuming she will marry and might leave, the partners are more likely to select a different vice president this year, someone they are more convinced will stay with the firm.

In fact, she is not certain what she will do. She could commute to work from a new home in a different city. Her fiancé could move to her city. She may quit; she may stay. At this point she does not know. Serious career questions require serious thought and analysis, but her immediate concern was: "What do I do about wearing my engagement ring at the office?" Well, what would be wrong with wearing the ring on a chain around her neck under a layer of clothes and close to her heart? That satisfies the woman and her fiancé's desire to "wear the ring," and it keeps things private, out of "nosy peers' sight" until she can get clearer in her thinking and what she wants to do. Later, she can bring up the subject and handle it the way that is best for her. This is an intelligent woman, but the situation illustrates the value of getting additional perspective and of the kind of objectivity coaching is intended to provide. The co-coach becomes a watchdog, another pair of eyes.

The writer of westerns Louis L'Amour said it well, "Up to a point a man's life is shaped by environment, heredity, and movements and changes in the world about him; then there comes a time when it lies within his grasp to shape the clay of his life into the sort of thing he wishes to be. Only the weak blame parents, their race, their times, lack of good fortune, or the quirks of fate. Everyone has it within his power to say, this I am today, that I shall be tomorrow. The wish, however, must be implemented by deeds."

If you eliminate trepidation, apprehension, and hesitation from your life, and *add* an improved operating standard, manner, or system—technique—you significantly enhance your odds for success.

PERSONAL EMPOWERMENT . . . YOU'RE HERE, NOW WHAT?

There's a lot of talk from management currently about empowering employees. Don't wait until management gets around to it, *do it for yourself.* Power does not come from a job title, a prestigious employer name, the location of an office, or the size of a paycheck. Power does come from eliminating self-defeating activities, *and*:

- Managing an adequate attitude
- Maintaining physical comportment
- Using interpersonal finesse

Power is the marriage of style and substance. You know you have it when you can change how things are done in this world. That's personal empowerment. It's never too early to select and focus on the critical success factors required in business life. And it's never too late. Don't ever feel you've had your chance already, and it's gone now. It is not. Do it for your corporate life; do it for your personal life.

In the last year I've personally coached fifty different company presidents. You might think at that level, they know all they need to. They don't. At that level they can better see all they need to learn. One of them explained, "It's like you climb a mountain and all you see is the top of another mountain to climb." Every one of those company presidents would do okay in life without my coaching. After all, they've done pretty well to get where they are! But every one of them has discovered they will do *even better* with coaching. We all need a little self-tuning, tweaking, and polishing.

You've likely accomplished a great deal in your life—so far, perhaps more than you ever thought you could. But some things still eat at you. Certain people and situations may trigger you to lose self-control. Later you regret it, but at the time it's all-consuming. You know it has nothing to do with the work, you can do that easily, but it's the people. They are such a pain—subordinates, coworkers, managers. If it weren't for them, you'd be fine! No one gets away from these frustrations. Some are just better at dealing with it. I'll be talking to you like I talk to my clients, in the most practical, honest way I can. I've seen coaching make a remarkable difference in many people's lives and I'd like it to make a difference in yours. You are already a successful person or you wouldn't be reading this. You have everything it takes to be even more accomplished. (Chapter 3 will prove that to you.)

Quite frankly, reaching a goal is frequently due to luck, occasionally due to coincidence, and sometimes due to skill. With the right coaching, you can "turn skill on" for consistent success. The result will be one of those wonderful zones where everything is right with the world. That too is personal empowerment.

IT'S ALWAYS FUN TO HANDLE THINGS WELL, BUT EFFORT IS REQUIRED

Someone once told me that *memories are better than dreams*. Think about that. Remember at times when you've handled something really well. Isn't it more pleasant to *reflect* back on what you've done successfully than to dream about handling something satisfactorily? And it's fun. Think about when you gather with old chums from college, work, or the sports field. How does the conversation go?

> *"Remember when we . . ."*
> *"I'll never forget the time . . ."*
> *"Did I ever tell you about the time . . . "*

You seldom hear . . .

> *"Let's share our future plans . . . "*
> *"Something that may happen is . . ."*
> *"I want to tell you about the time I'm*
> *(we're) going to have . . ."*

Of course not. Memories *are* better than dreams. But it takes effort (and activity) to make memories, effort in eliminating fear and improving your technique. The good part of exertion is that any small change you make today will change your entire future forever. The biggest test of your courage may be letting go of the things that hold you back, and that takes effort. Tour de France winning cyclist Greg LeMond says, "I have always struggled to achieve excellence. One thing that cycling has taught me is that if you can achieve something without a struggle, it's not going to be satisfying."

If you wait for the "right" time to start intense effort on yourself, you'll wait forever. There will never be a better time than now. Waiting will only cause you to miss opportunities. In business and in life, to be successful, you have to give 110 percent. This book is

47

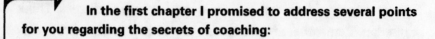

In the first chapter I promised to address several points for you regarding the secrets of coaching:

1. Questions you need to ask yourself
2. Tools to fit the job at hand
3. The variety of targets possible
4. Strategy to go forward
5. Fall-back plans

Next we'll move into the how-to-make-this happen-for-you part of the book, where I'll deliver on that promise.

Chapter 3 enables you to start the process. It will help you unearth your tools, and that's an exciting discovery. By getting a clear picture of yourself as you are now, you can create the picture of where you're going. As Lily Tomlin says, "All my life I've always wanted to be somebody, but I see now I should have been more specific." Together, you and I, are going to get very specific, because we're going to create some great memories in our lives.

your extra 10 percent. It's not where you stand in life today, it's where you're moving to today and tomorrow that makes life fun. Ask yourself where you want to go, is it attainable, will you make the necessary sacrifice, have you laid out how you'll get there, will the payoff be worth it, do you have what it takes, can you keep at it, how is your competition, what will hold you back, can you overcome it, and will it make you happy? If you seriously answer each question, you'll have to conclude that this will take some energy. But in a sense, you already have everything it will take, if properly channeled.

I enjoy and appreciate hearing from clients how wonderful a coaching session has been. But I can't help following up with a tough question: "Okay, now what are you going to do differently tomorrow?" I'll be equally hard on you because the world is hard. Life will ask more of you than I possibly could. There is nothing worse than going down in defeat and not having used all your tools. That makes for very bad memories.

NOTES

1. I have been a guest lecturer at this MBA program and I must tell you, young, inexperienced MBAs are the most difficult to coach. Why? They haven't failed enough yet. Give me someone with significant setbacks and I'll give you a successfully coachable individual capable of doing great things in life.

2. Another time waster is being a follower.

CEO COACHING TECHNIQUES YOU CAN APPLY YOURSELF

No one will ever know you better than yourself. No one cares more about you and your advancement than yourself. To be coached—*to be your own coach*—you must want it. You must be *ready* in your life. You're ready when you know there is more to your existence than what you are currently doing. To be more productive, prosperous, and even *personally peaceful*—you must want to have it. You're ready when you accept that you may need to alter your mindset, learn new approaches, and even change behavior big-time. It will take tremendous effort on your part. But you will also find tremendous joy in the wonderful feeling of handling things well and of winning.

A few years into my career I concluded that I needed to make some shifts in my mindset, approach, and behavior. After a thorough self-review, which reminded me of my curiosity about "chiefs," I decided I had to understand how business really runs, from the top down. In my short time in the working world I had discovered it wasn't like I thought it was going to be, thought it should be, or even the way it was taught in school. I also realized I was many, many years away from getting to the top and therefore truly understanding it. So I decided to coach myself in the "ways at the top" before I got there, so maybe I'd get there sooner!

CEO APPRENTICE

I made a conscious decision to apprentice with company presidents and CEOs. In my chosen profession that level was the one I wanted to understand most. Had I been in the ministry maybe I'd have tried to apprentice with a bishop or archbishop. Had it been sports, I might have chosen an Olympic athlete. But in business it was the president/CEO position. In the beginning I sought out meetings with "successful" people in all areas of business life and asked how they achieved their success. After I acquired some skill and self-assurance, I concentrated on presidents and CEOs. In subsequent years I've totaled over 4000 people interviewed. This week, I'll add another one or two. (Last week, I added politician Jack Kemp—on a flight.)

If you want to learn how to be a gang member, you hang around with a gang. If you want to learn how to rock climb, you hang around with rock climbers. If you want to learn about presidents and CEOs, you hang around with them. Part of the secret of coaching CEOs, executives, or anyone interested in getting better is to learn to understand the language and look like you belong there. When they see how you handle yourself, they conclude that you "fit" in, and the entire thing becomes a positive cycle. You look and act the part, they think you belong, invite you in, you're in, and you learn to act the part even more. Many of the people you're in awe of today will become friends, so you'll do social things together. Just like them, you too can participate in politics or charities. Perhaps your professional work can bring you deeper and deeper into their inner circle. The point is to get around the best and emulate the best of the best.

If you think this sounds a little calculating, stop. (I prefer to call it strategic.) You do the same thing every day of your life. You try to fit in with a:

- New company—from learning and following the company culture to using the company pen.

- New team—by wearing the team uniform and drinking at their hangout.

- New community—by attending the town fair and shopping where the locals do.

- New church—by volunteering to be an usher or baking cookies for the bakesale.

If you're smart, you act as if you belong, and they accept you as if you do.

You can do the same thing in any aspect of your professional life. For a certain period of time, just limit your audience, and therefore time, to the presidents and CEOs of the world, or anyone you want to better understand and deal with more effectively. How do you get to meet these people? You research who would be interesting and valuable to meet and contact them. Sometimes you'll hear about an individual from someone else, read about someone in a magazine or newspaper, or simply run into a person in the course of business. At times it takes a degree of courage, creativity, and some salesmanship to convince prominent people to give you a little bit of their time.

On average, one in five of those you contact "out of the blue" will see you. It will demand lots of tenacity on your part because you don't just make five calls and obtain one appointment. Sometimes you initiate 25 contacts and receive no appointments. Then the next day, three, four, maybe five will come through. It feels glorious when that happens. You need to go into conversations with organized questions and a specific purpose. Your goal must be to never leave without learning something new and helpful for your quest. Frequently, the person will see your sincerity to learn from others and introduce you to a friend or associate, which saves five cold contacts on your part.

I've landed a few "freebies" in just this way. In a meeting with former Senator Gary Hart, he suggested I meet designer Ralph Lauren. During conversations with the CEO of Fruit of the Loom, he introduced me to the Governor of Kentucky. At a conference in California, Richard Torrenzano, then Senior Vice President of the New York Stock Exchange enabled me to meet Don Hewitt, producer of "60 Minutes." The best way to meet Mr. or Ms. Bigs is through other Mr. and Ms. Bigs.[1]

START, CONTINUE, BUT NEVER COMPLETE YOUR SELF-COACHING

It's most important to realize your development can never end. On the plus side, what you need to work on is simple, not complex. It's honest and real. It's also not exactly the way you'd like it to be all of the time. But you can choose to understand what you need to work on and deal with it or not understand it, not deal with it, and not achieve the success you are capable of. Because your life is complicated, you might feel a complicated approach to self-coaching is required. Not so. A simple solution works. It does require a degree of self-review though.

This chapter lays out the same self-review steps you would go through in an expensive coaching session. The only difference is that you're the coach, you can do it on your own schedule, and the cost is pure *effort,* with very little out-of-pocket expense. Another important thing to know is that every bit of exertion you put into coaching yourself will make for a bigger "career life-preserver." And since you plan to swim in some deep water in your life, you want it as big as possible!

So here are three rules that will guide you during your self-coaching journey:

Rule 1. **Remember, you're not alone in this.** Take comfort in knowing that most people spend their careers working on the same issues and problems you work on. I've worked on them. The people I apprenticed with worked on them. The people I coach work on them. "Working on them" means doing, not just knowing. A lot of things discussed in this book you already know. The difference between you and others is what you choose to do with it. "The quality of a person's life is in direct proportion to their commitment to excellence, regardless of the chosen field or endeavor," said late Green Bay Packer coach Vince Lombardi.

Your success will be in direct proportion to your commitment to your self-review and to better self-coaching.

Rule 2. **Don't be extreme; be consistent.** The secret to success in self-coaching is *constancy*, constancy with a good purpose and technique. The ancient philosopher Helvetius wrote, "Genius is nothing but continued attention." You can't just do the "right" thing every once in a while. You have to do it all the time. After you experience profitable and productive results, you'll agree it's all worth it.

Rule 3. **Be self-disciplined.** Discipline is fun. It rewards you with the greatest feeling. Think about when you've used it and how good it felt, like when you've worked really hard the last few days, had several meetings, put out numerous fires, and are finally home. It's the time of day you'd typically go to the gym, but you're just beat. Nevertheless, you discipline yourself to go. You work out, kind of slow in the beginning, but then you get a surge of energy and find yourself doing a record number (for you at least) of laps or lifts or whatever. Don't you just feel great? Aren't you pleased with yourself? Don't you walk out with pride about your discipline, strength of character, and constitution? Of course you do. Well that's the kind of temerity required for your self-coaching.

Take consolation in the fact that everyone (who's any good) works on their self-development all of the time. The successful ones are consistent and self-disciplined—starting with their self-review. You're a thinking adult. You know (or will learn) your tendencies, reactions, and behaviors through the exercises provided here. Once you know, it does not give you the license to succumb to them, but to rise above them.

Three-time superbowl player and Denver Bronco Bill Romanowski says, "Since I was 10 years old, whenever I was at a party or doing any activity, a little voice in my head would ask, 'Will this keep me from getting in the NFL?'" If he concluded it might hinder his goal, he didn't do it. That's self-discipline and constancy. And the truth is, we all have a similar "little voice." The key is to listen to it more of the time.

GET READY TO SIZE-UP YOURSELF

I know you know yourself pretty well, but you're worth knowing yourself *really* well. To do that, you need to examine what you've done and what you're like at this point in time. We'll do it in three parts:

1. Your story.

2. Thoughts about yourself.

3. 360 degree point of view.

SELF-REVIEW PART 1: WRITE YOUR LIFE STORY

Literally, write your life story: where you were born, grew up, work your parents did, memorable moments in grade school, high school, college, successes, setbacks along the way, why you chose your career, how you got to where you are, and where you want to go. Why is writing your background so very important?

- It gets you thinking in an organized manner.
- It refreshes your memory of where you've been and all you've done.
- You feel good when you think back and reflect (or bad, if you haven't worked very hard).
- You end up with more complete information for updating a résumé and job interviewing.
- You discover patterns and tendencies.
- You reveal gaps.

As close as you are to you, you can forget unless you write it down!

By the way, this written history could make a wonderful present for your children someday. Think about it. Wouldn't it be interesting to have your own parent's story in such detail?

To do Part 1 well will take some time. You may want to buy a special notebook or create a new computer file to start collecting answers to the questions asked in this section, but I've left some space in this book for you to jot down some answers, too. I suggest you work on this a little every day (starting today) and then finish it up over a long weekend. You can do it on a mountain, on a boat, at the beach, or any place your thinking is clear and focused.

Here is an array of questions to get you thinking as you tell your tale. Give as much detail as you can remember. Don't worry about grammar and syntax at this point, just get the information documented in some tangible form.

THE EARLY YEARS

When and where were you born?

What was your relationship with other children in the family?

What kind of work did your parents do?

What religion were you raised in?

What do you remember about grade school? How about junior high or middle school?

What was your relationship with your parents like?

What do you remember about high school?

Were you popular? With what types of kids?

Does anything stand out that was life shaping?

THE MIDDLE YEARS

Were any of your teachers or coaches particularly memorable? Who? Why?

Did you work after school?

What did you think you wanted to be when you grew up?

How did you choose what college to go to (or not go to)?

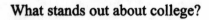

What did you study? What were you going to be?

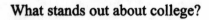

What stands out about college?

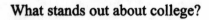

CHAPTER THREE

Did you pay for college yourself? How?

What kind of work did you do during college?

UP TO THE PRESENT

What was your first job after college (or graduate school)?

What was your first boss like?

How did you do?

When and why did you change jobs?

How were your relationships with bosses, peers, subordinates?

When did you first manage people?

How did you learn how to do that?

What were the circumstances of getting (or losing) each succeeding job up to your current job?

Where/how did you meet your spouse/significant other?

What kind of work does that person do?

What do you do for fun?

What creates passion for you?

What brings you to the point in your career that you want coaching?

What do you want to get out of coaching?

Where are you going in your life, both personally and professionally?

Where should you be going?

FOR NOW AND LATER

If you didn't have to worry about money, what would you do at this point in your career?

Besides money, what is keeping you from doing it?

What causes people doing your work to leapfrog ahead of peers?

What keeps people on the bench?

What's been your shining moment to date?

What advice have you been given?

Did you take it? Why or why not?

What skills do you want to work on?

What talents do you want to develop?

What's holding you back?

What have you learned from life so far?

Those are your story-writing questions. Don't skimp on your answers or skip over things. Depending on your experience, a certain question may go many levels deeper than how I've laid it out, so look for ways to dig deeper. For example, the question about your first job after college might generate the following kinds of questions and take you into more levels of detail:

How did you get the job?

Who interviewed you?

Did he or she do an accurate job in selling the position?

What was the best part of the job; the worst part?

What did you learn from it?

In hindsight, was it a good first job?

Do you stay in touch with your first mentor from that job?

What Patterns Might You Have Inherited?

This next part of your history requires help from your parents, as-suming they're available. You can give them the list to answer, read the list to them and ask for their answers, or if you find the direct approach uncomfortable, you can casually weave them into your conversation over time. (The latter is the least desirable, of course, because it takes longer to complete.)

YOUR PARENTS' WORK HISTORY

What was your first job?

What are your earliest recollections of bosses?

How did people describe you?

What did your bosses say about you?

What were your talents?

What were your skills?

What were your fears?

What were your goals?

YOUR PARENTS' SUCCESSES

What is your best story about a job change or promotion?

What is the best story people told about you?

What was your greatest victory or shining moment?

What attracted you to the company, job, or career you chose?

What was the biggest surprise you discovered?

What was the best advice you received?

What words still ring in your ears?

What was the best scheme you ever carried out?

YOUR PARENTS' SETBACKS

What's your biggest regret?

What do you wish you'd spent time on?

What was difficult for you?

What do you wish you'd done differently?

What advice do you remember being given that you didn't take?

What was your most embarrassing moment?

THE BIG ONE

What have you learned from life?

Your parents give you an interesting perspective on things. You might be shocked at the similarity in experiences and feelings when it comes to business. The very least you will get out of this is communication unlike what you typically have with the people who raised you. You can see this isn't a two-hour project—maybe two hours the first day! If you're going into sufficient detail, it may take an hour for each major question. But this may be a once-in-a-lifetime exercise, so do it right.

Discovering patterns is the most important reason for this work. When I did a written history for myself several years ago, I saw several patterns. One was my tolerance (or preference) for solo activities. Sportswise, I enjoy windsurfing, swimming, walking, hiking, and cross-country skiing. There's not a team sport on the list. I'm competitive, yes, but in solo sports. I enjoy being with myself instead of with other people. My early jobs during high school and college involved direct sales. I was a solo "producer." As I wrote before, my parents had their own business during my formative years. I've been self-employed for well over twenty years. Looking at my patterns, it becomes rather obvious that I'm not a corporate-type team-player. So how do you look for patterns from your story, i.e., life history?

When the choice was totally up to you, what did you do?

Try to isolate the activities you had to do versus what you took upon yourself to do. Maybe you *had* to go to bible school classes in the summer of your thirteenth year, but you *chose* to organize a softball team during recess. And the softball team became so big that you ended up forming several teams. Then you talked the teachers into letting the kids wear T-shirts with the name the "Bible Bombers" printed on the back. At the end of the bible school session, when they had the traditional picnic, you organized a softball tournament and sold lemonade to the parents who came to watch.

Or perhaps during college on spring break you discovered you liked to sail, but you didn't have the money to have your own boat. So you started a sailing club because you figured if you could get a group of similarly interested people, someone would have a boat you could crew on. Enough interest was generated that you organized a regatta, printed up T-shirts for sale, got sponsors to provide Pepsi free of charge but sold the bags of Frito-Lays for a profit.

Looking for patterns does not mean being so literal that you conclude from the above examples that you are an "athlete" who should be in the T-shirt manufacturing or soft-drink business. The examples could indicate that you like to be outdoors doing physical activity, enjoy competition, can organize groups of people, can sell your ideas to "higher-ups," are willing to risk taking on new ventures, are willing to take on a leadership role, and have enough sense to try to make some money along the way.

Did you do things to exercise your brain or your body?

In your life, when you had the choice, did you go to a book to read or head into the woods for a hike with your dog? After your first job, when you discovered you didn't like selling in the heartland, your parents let you move home to job hunt. Instead, you spent an entire year living off your savings reading biographies of world leaders, histories of countries, and political science books. You got up in the morning, exercised, then sat and read until dinnertime. You read every single book in these three categories available at your local library, plus all the magazines and newspapers with a similar topical bent. In one article you learned about a new think tank being formed in Washington, D.C. and you applied. You didn't get the job so you volunteered to work for free.

Some of the patterns displayed here are: you don't give in to peer pressure of what one is "supposed" to do, you like to read to gain information on your own more than having others tell you things, you obviously have an interest in the political world supported with knowledge of history, you like to think about and digest things, and you have understanding and supportive parents. From a coaching perspective, there is a good chance you are more intellectually energized than emotionally so you're more likely to need work on your people skills.

Did you do the things you did with people or on your own?

In the preceding examples I was writing about two different clients. The first one preferred organizing, motivating, and leading groups of people. The second person preferred not being around people and focused instead on organizing and motivating himself.

Other questions you can ask yourself to find patterns:

When was I happiest or most relaxed?

What kinds of people do I tend to seek out as friends, associates, mentors?

Who has taught me the most?

Do I listen and take advice from others?

Do I like to learn in isolation or in a group?

What has been important to me in life?

Where (geographically) have I found the most satisfaction?

When have I been most productive, after a setback or after a success?

How have I changed or not changed?

What subjects or words pop up most frequently in my history?

The key to remember is that your story is where you've been, not necessarily where you're going. This means you first identify tendencies, then you can set goals or "triggers" to get you where you *could* be.

Another important thing to understand is that discovering patterns does not mean giving yourself an excuse, "I'm this way and that's the way it is." Instead, it means, "Now that I see *why* I'm like this, I can choose to do something about it." That's why I took on the CEO apprentice work. I knew I needed to understand corporate life inside and out, all the way up the ladder. I had to fill in the gaps that a self-employed career path would have. Similarly, when you see your own patterns and tendencies, you'll be able to enhance the good stuff and downplay the not-so-good. Then you *make* your future—regardless of your history.

SELF-REVIEW PART 2: THOUGHTS ABOUT YOURSELF

If I asked you to tell me what you think about yourself, you'd probably say something like, "I'm a happy, healthy person, fairly ambitious, and anxious to make my mark on the world." Or you might say, "I'm fairly frustrated with life. Things haven't turned out like I thought. I worry about my health, my family's future, and my career progress." Either way, you haven't told me a lot of substantive stuff. Both comments could be said by anyone at any given time. So to get more substance into these exercises, the questions about yourself have to be asked in a more imaginative way, so here is a fun way to look at why you are like you are (or at least why you think you are).

There are two sections. The first is to complete the sentence. The second is to explain in a sentence why you selected the answer you did:

1. The question: If I were a _____, what would I be?

   • If I were a **fruit**, what would I be?

• If I were a **job,** what would I be?

• If I were the **weather**, what would I be?

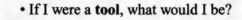

• If I were a **tool**, what would I be?

- If I were a **temperature**, what would I be?

- If I were an **animal**, what would I be?

• If I were a **smell**, what would I be?

• If I were a **crime**, what would I be?

• If I were a **toy**, what would I be?

• If I were **something to wear**, what would I be?

• If I were a **country**, what would I be?

• If I were **spare time activity**, what would I be?

• If I were a **sound,** what would I be?

• If I were a **time of day**, what would I be?

• If I were a **department in the supermarket**, what would I be?

2. You will get 15 questions. Answer each question and briefly explain your answer.

Here's how one person answered the questions and the reason why:

If I were a *fruit,* what would I be?
A persimmon. It is rare. Few know of it. It is unlike any other fruit. It's extremely good. And it can be used in a humble pudding recipe.

If I were a *job,* what would I be?
A beautician. The job makes other people look and feel good.

If I were *weather*, what would I be?
Clear and sunny. It represents calm and clear.

If I were a *tool,* what would I be?
A ratchet screwdriver. With little effort, a lot is accomplished. It wields a lot of power.

If I were a *temperature,* what would I be?
98.6. Because that's normal.

If I were an *animal*, what would I be?
A lion. It has power even without roaring.

If I were a *smell*, what would I be?
Clean. Because clean is pure and simple.

If I were a *crime*, what would I be?
Counterfeiting. I often fear being found out in my job.

If I were a *toy*, what would I be?
Etch-a-Sketch™. I can create what I want, erase it, and do it again.

If I were *something to wear*, what would I be?
Best suit of clothes. Because it's something I feel proud of myself in.

If I were a *country*, what would I be?
The U.S. It was founded for good reasons. It is the world leader. We make mistakes. We recover and thrive.

If I were a *sparetime activity*, what would I be?
Chess. It requires thought, consideration of others, a poker face, and luck.

If I were a *sound*, what would I be?
A familiar, pleasant voice. Because it's something familiar that puts a smile on your face when you hear it and recognize it.

If I were a *time of day*, what would I be?
2:00 PM. It's nondescript.

If I were a *department in a supermarket*, what would I be?
The health food section. Because I'm good for your health.

Here's what that line of self-questioning and explanation says about this particular person: The individual likes the out-of-the-ordinary and takes personal pride in feeling unique. She cares about others like she cares about herself. She trys to keep calm in crisis and maintain an affable demeanor in general.

She likes power and wants to be efficient and productive. Although she likes to feel special, she knows she's pretty typical of most human beings—normal. She doesn't want to be loud, obnoxious, or arrogant, and she values clarity, simplicity, and straightforwardness. She has a certain amount of self-doubt—"not wanting to be found out." She knows she makes mistakes but is also careful to correct them. She feels pride in her accomplishments, understands the "game" she's playing (like we all are playing), and she wants to play it better—but in a fair way. In general, she wants to do good.

This is not an attempt at deep psychological analysis. It is, however, an interesting way to look at how you think about yourself. And it's just a cool tool to help you decide what gaps you might want to eliminate and what strengths you might want to reaffirm and enhance.

SELF-REVIEW PART 3: 360 DEGREE POINT OF VIEW

Up to this point we've looked at sizing yourself up. Now let's have others do it. We're not going to randomly ask people for opinions, but will instead seek feedback in a deliberate, organized fashion. You need to learn how you're viewed by others so you can take action to change the view if necessary. Be open to the results in this exercise. Be careful not to become defensive. You can approach this formally or informally. Formally would mean utilizing a form similar to those typically available from most human resources departments. With those forms you follow a formal sequence:

1. Get agreement from your manager, peers, and direct reports to complete the survey.

2. Collect and compile the survey, utilizing the human resources coordinator.

3. Review your survey summary with the human resources person to gain consensus and perspective on strengths and needs.

4. Set up a development plan.

5. Share the results with the 360 participants.

Participants will be answering questions about your business competence, results, analytical thinking, organizational savvy, impact, leadership, and professional maturity. Typically, the formal process has a "standard norm" against which you are evaluated. Most have you complete the same material that the 360 participants do so you can compare your self-analysis against their view.

When you receive the formal findings, look for consistencies, patterns, general trends, top strengths and weaknesses, development opportunities, and big surprises.

Then ask yourself three questions:

• Is the feedback accurate?

• Is it important?

• Do I want to change?

If you can't (or choose not) to go through the computerized testing, you can gather fairly accurate results informally—if you stay organized and disciplined. Select your target people. Ask for their honest, straightforward thinking. Pose specific questions to each. Here's a list of issues to work with.

• How well do I look for ways to meet or exceed customer needs?

• How well do I look for ways to meet or exceed management's needs?

- How well do I take a positive approach to business?
- How well do I work effectively with people in a wide variety of circumstances?
- How well do I analyze complex situations accurately and in a timely manner?
- How well do I minimize activities that do not add value to the organization?
- How well do I value others' thinking; champion others' thoughts?
- How well do I understand how to get things done in the organization?
- How well do I have in-depth industry knowledge?
- How well do I overcome obstacles?
- How well do I quickly act when I see an opportunity?
- How well do I demonstrate intellectual curiosity?
- How well do I make sure I can be counted on?
- How well do I remain in control when stressed or pressed?
- How well do I gain trust?
- How well do I admit responsibility for failures or mistakes?
- How well do I help others?
- How well do I follow through to get results?
- How well do I set a good example?
- How well do I see and understand the broad view of business.

If you don't choose to do 360 formally or informally, at least surmise what people you work with are thinking. You can do this simple check. Pick 10 people you deal with today. Five of them should rank higher than you, five at your peer level or below. Take out a full sheet of paper and down the left side of the paper space out the 10 names. Across the top of the page list three columns titles: YES, NO, DON'T KNOW. Now, alongside each name, place a check appropriate to that person's answer to this question: "Does this individual see me as competent, memorable, impressive, credible, genuine, trusted, and liked?"

Obviously your goal is all YES responses. By the way, DON'T KNOW equals NO. The people who checked NO and DON'T KNOW are your "assignment" people, i.e., the people you need to work on to upgrade their opinion of you. The problem with asking others to evaluate you is that they lie, not always, but sometimes. The ones below you tend to speak a tad more favorably about you than they really feel. After all, you are their boss. You do have power over them (at least in their eyes). People above you tend to be a bit more negative than they really feel. It seems they feel compelled to "constructively criticize," partly because they want to remind you that you need improvement and you aren't nearly ready for their job, in case that's what you're thinking. Peers tend to do both, for some of the same reasons.

Regardless of the approach you take to hear from others, get as much input as possible, test what you hear, offer your perspective, but don't be defensive. Then set aside areas you want to work on and how you plan to address them. (Chapters 4, 5, and 6 are intended to help you do this very thing.)

That's it for your private brainstorming session! The three parts require a lot of work, it's true, but now you have an "industrial strength" self-review. You've reviewed how you got where you are, along with the successes and setbacks that you learned from. You've examined influences and influencers from inside and outside the home. You've scrutinized what you think about yourself and allowed others to assess you as well. From all this self-inspection, you now should be able to isolate trigger situations that you want to work on to continue your professional growth and development. Here's where the fun begins.

ISOLATE TRIGGERS THAT SET YOU OFF AND SET GOALS TO HANDLE THEM

You and I handle most things pretty well, but some situations derail us, at least temporarily. Those incidents are "triggers." From all the introspection you've gone through, sort out your triggers. As your co-coach, I can recommend some common triggers, or patterns of behavior many people need work on. They include:

- Altering attitudes
- Improving physical presence
- Increasing capacity for boldness

The specific trigger incidents become the basis for your development plan. "Development plan" is another way of saying your "goals." When attacking your triggers, I recommend you follow the "2-to-1 rule": *For the amount of time it takes to do something, spend twice that amount of time thinking about it first.* Fact is, if you do one thing right a day, in a year you will have done 365 things right! (The same goes for one thing wrong a day.)

Your Goals

Ever hitchhike? Friends of mine have. They tell me you get more rides if you show a sign of where you're going. That's goal-setting. My friends also say that while you're holding your thumb out, walk in the direction you're going. Then at the end of the day, if you didn't get a lift, you're still closer to your destination. Having goals, plans, and dreams is nice. But unless you do something about them every day—several times a day—they'll continue to be goals, plans, and dreams, not reality.

From your triggers, target key areas for development, and write them in an action-oriented statement:

- Increase positive exposure in my company.

- Get a new account each month.

- Become a good speaker.

- Polish my professional presence.

- Increase my salary.

- Get a new job.

- Perform beyond my bosses' expectations on XYZ project.

Chapters 4, 5, and 6 provide more specific practices to help you attack goals.

Train Your Brain

Write down your goals. Put them into a succinct sentence. Then write that statement down 15 times a day, every day. When Scott Adams, creator of the "Dilbert" books, wanted to leave his middle management position at Pacific Bell, he wrote, "I will be a syndicated cartoonist," *15* times a day. Later the self-talk became more bold, "I will become the best cartoonist on the planet." Today, Adams's cartoon strip is carried in 1700 newspapers in 51 countries, and he gets $30,000 for a speaking engagement! He admits he doesn't know exactly how it works other than, "You'll observe things happening that will make that objective more likely to happen." He's tried the "15 times" routine in impressing a certain woman, a GMAT test score, and getting his chief rivals to retire. The affirmation approach worked every time, he says.

What writing a goal 15 times a day does is bring your desire to the conscious level at least 15 times that day. Unless you force yourself to think and write your target, you can easily go a day and forget to consciously think about it! Then you forget the next day and the next day. Finally, on day four you remember and think about it one time. Honestly, how much effort has been put in toward the goal over the four days if you've seriously thought about it only once?

Instead, if you've deliberately reminded yourself to write down your main aim all those times (a time or two before breakfast, a couple before lunch, several throughout the afternoon, wrapped up with the final five or six just before bedtime), it will more likely happen. If you forget today altogether, which does happen, you have to do 30 the next day. If you've forgotten two days in a row, then you have to write 45 on the third day. Did you ever have to write something 100 times on the chalk board after school? I did. On various days Sister Agnes made me write:

I will not talk in class.

I will not forget my homework.

I will not hit Mary Ann.

I will not run in the hallways.

In hindsight, I don't think Sister Agnes liked me very much. Interesting thing though, after writing one of those statements 100 times, I didn't commit that transgression again. There must have been some benefit to writing! Jeff Neppl, a vice president at Campbell's, is a friend of mine. We were talking about this and he said he had to write *I will not talk in class* so often that he'd write extra pages so when the teacher told him to write, he'd just whip out some prewritten ones to satisfy her. It's not the act of writing that causes results, of course. Once you've thought about something, you'll likely see an opportunity to *act* on it, all the more if you write it down.

Remember Rule 3: Self-discipline creates habit. Any act repeated becomes a habit and then it becomes easy, and you usually end up taking pleasure in it. That encourages you to perform the good behavior more frequently and therefore reinforces it to become habit. You see, people are bundles of habits and habits have greater force than reason. Pro golfer Lee Trevino says of repetition: "There is no such thing as a natural touch. Touch is something you create by hitting a million golf balls." If you try this, and I hope you will, you'll find it does take effort and discipline. If you can't discipline yourself to do the simple act of writing your goal, how can you hope to *act* on your goal. If you spend an amount of time every day thinking about something persistently, you're bound to be ahead of most everyone else.

Bob Bozeman, former CEO of USonline, carefully puts a folded sheet of paper inside his shirt pocket every day. He has for as many years as he can remember. Why? One of his goals is to add two people to his network of contacts a day. When he meets or learns of someone new, he uses the paper to write that person's name and then later transfers the names and information from the paper to his database. Bob has buillt a successful career by his consistency. Besides having run companies and lobbying in Washington, he was hired for a three-year project to rebuild Dallas's image after the Kennedy assassination. The daily contacts he has made have meant a great deal to his career. Dreaming doesn't cut it. For example, you can't sustain the goal of losing weight, even if you've written it 15 times a day, in between eating Twinkies. Actions and desires must corroborate each other. There is an old Chinese saying, "Any man who could concentrate for as much as three minutes on any given problem could rule the world." The writing exercise keeps your focus in view. If they aren't "in writing" and "in your face" all of the time, they aren't goals, only wishes.

Questions to ask yourself

- Am I ready to get some coaching?
- Do I understand and appreciate the importance?
- Will I put in the required effort?
- Do I see the simplicity versus the complexity required?
- Will I keep at it, even when stifled?

The answer should be "yes" to all of the above.

Tools to fit the job at hand

- Seek solace in the fact you're not alone in these efforts. You have me to help.
- Everyone who goes anywhere has a coach, even if it is herself or himself.
- It's more important to be consistent than extreme in your efforts.
- If you've got the self-discipline, use if for yourself.
- Complete your written version of your life story. Set it aside for a week. Reread it with fresh eyes. Look for patterns of successes and setbacks. Write them down.
- Complete your self-review of personal motivation. Set it aside for a week. Reread it with fresh eyes. Look for patterns and write them down.
- Complete your 360-degree point of review. Set it aside for a week. Reread it with fresh eyes. Look for patterns and write them down.

- List the problematic areas you discovered in the preceding three activities.

- Attach goals to those areas.

  Train your brain 15 times a day toward each goal.

The variety of targets possible:

- Understanding politics and managing upwards.

- Learning to stop fighting the battle after the war is over.

- Developing more self-confidence to step out of your comfort zone.

- Learning to do the right thing in the right way versus the right thing in the wrong way.

- Cultivating more executive maturity.

- Learning how to establish a comfortable presence that attracts followers.

- Earning the respect of management.

Strategy to go forward: Managing Upwards[2]

- First and foremost, do exemplary work. Have a solid reason to want management to pay attention to you as well as a solid reason why they will want to.

- Quantify your contributions and let the right people know. If it's fact, you are not tooting your own horn but rather making it easier for the boss to understand your work.

- In a succinct, clear manner, state the situation, explain what you did, and report the results. This can be done on e-mail, on the phone, in a note, or in the hallway. Just make sure you do it consistently.

- Try to share credit wherever you can. Enthusiastically and sincerely ask, "How did you do that?" You might learn something valuable.

- See possibilities, not limitations, in making sure your accomplishments get noticed in an appropriate way.

- Raise your positive visibility by *real acts* that produce results management wants. (Allow your name to be put in for committee chairs, join business or trade groups, volunteer to be a company or industry spokesperson, apply for awards, share the spotlight with others, write an article for a company publication, get involved in community events, and so forth.)

- Get a reputation that supports the way you want to be perceived.

- Use theatrics, "fake it before you make it" if necessary. (Just be careful not to fake competence, results, values, integrity, and other critical things.)

- Get a reputation for being quick to "get up to speed" on things.

- Size up the boss. Find out how he or she views results, recognition, praise, power, personal integrity, communication, family, etc. Find out by asking.

- Ask questions in an inquisitive manner, not an interrogatory manner. Ask. Observe. Ask more.

- Give what the boss wants in the way she wants it.

- Be alert to changes in her situation.

- If you are really smart in managing relationships upward, you will keep people apprised of what you have done or are about to do.

- Don't be afraid to say "no" even to superiors. If you take on too much and end up doing poor work, missing deadlines, or burning out, you'll both lose. It's a good idea when you say no to someone to give the person something in exchange that you can and will do. For example, "No, I can't take on project X, but I will help Joe complete project Y."

Fall-back plans

- Do not think that good work will speak for itself. It should, but it doesn't.

- Pay attention to how your boss and your boss's boss handle themselves physically. How do they dress? What symbols of power do they have around them?

- Observe what types of people they surround themselves with? (Your boss may have a dismal presence himself but expect something else from others.)

- Take on the corporate traits you observe. Consistency is important if you choose this route, for example, staying late or coming in early, or sending thank you notes and letters of praise—with sincerity, of course.

- Acknowledge others (upwards) the way you would like to be acknowledged by them.

- Do a little today, a little next week, and keep at it. The secret to getting ahead is getting started.

- The bottom line: Do something unexpected but deeply desired by your boss.

NOTES

1. My interest in the Mr. Bigs came at an early age for a number of reasons: My parents had their own business when I was growing up so they were the "president/CEO" of their own thing and sort of extra special in the town of 5000 people where we lived. They ran their own show. They didn't have a boss like other kids' parents. I liked that.

Second, at age 13 I was reading a book that stated "the stars of tomorrow will be 'pink' collar workers," i.e., career-women. As a young girl, I had concluded I wasn't pretty enough to be a movie star, so a "business star" was a good alternative. Note: I didn't want to be a business worker, but a business star. To do that I figured I had to be at the top.

And third, my introduction to the first real and important organizational president I had ever met turned out to be good, and not so good. I'll tell you the story:

My aunt was his executive secretary and while visiting her I got to meet him. He was an imposing figure personally, tall and robust. He drove a new Cadillac and owned a private plane in which he took my father and me in to check out one of his cattle ranches. He loaned us his 54-foot cabin cruiser for a week's vacation on the lake. He gave me unlimited dimes to feed into the soda machine. To a young person, he seemed pretty important—a real Mr. Big!

One day I was spending time with my aunt at her office and she let me have the run of the place. I went into the president's office. Pretending to be him, I shut the door, sat in his big leather chair, and swirled around for a while.

To my total shock, hanging on the back of his door were plastic molds of various shaped women's breasts. I had never seen anything like that in my life! I had no idea anything like that could be made. (Obviously, this would not happen in today's business world, but this was back in the late 1960s.) I immediately left the office and went and sat on the front steps in total confusion. How could someone so nice, important, smart, and successful have such a shocking thing? (And no, this man was not in the breast implant business.)

Quite frankly, the combination of events intrigued me about the world of business—at the top. There was something noticeably different, but it stayed just beyond interpretation. So I decided to apprentice with CEOs, even though most didn't know I was doing it.

2. In each chapter I have selected one of the most prevalent problem areas clients experience and developed a suggested Strategy to Go Forward and a Fall-Back Plan. You, the reader, can "coach yourself" by using the Tools at Hand to attack any or all of the Variety of Targets, i.e., your trigger list, as you progress through your self-directed program.

USING MENTAL ENERGY: ATTITUDE MANAGEMENT

Managing your attitude is the heart of coaching. Everything starts in the mind. It is the foundation. The mind—*your mind*—must be under control because once you've *thought something* it can't be unthought. Franklin D. Roosevelt said, "Men are not prisoners of fate, but only prisoners of their own minds." For coaching purposes, managing means to empty your mind of limiting, destructive, disruptive, negative, nonproductive thoughts. Toss away any distracted, obsessive moods. Viacom's Sumner Redstone says, "Great successes are built on taking the negatives in your life and turning them around."

I had a car service whose driver was particularly skilled take me to New York's La Guardia Airport. He smoothly manipulated the vehicle to avoid a reckless driver and miss some debris on the road. I complimented him on his ability. He said, "For my vacation every year I fly to Germany, rent a Porsche, and drive the Autobahn for a week." I told him, "I used to own a Porsche 911 SC but sold it during tight financial times. I really hated to have to do that. I miss that car." He responded, "At least you were lucky to own one in your lifetime. Most of us will never have that. " Now *that's* attitude management, *choosing* a productive, constructive, versus a destructive perspective. Comedian George Carlin demonstrates a form of attitude management in his inimitable way: "Have you ever noticed? Anybody going slower than you is an idiot, and anyone faster than you is a maniac." A more positive variation on this theme comes from one of Hollywood's beauties, Michelle Pfeiffer, who says, "Somewhere along the line, I made the switch and was able to look at the bright side as opposed to the dark side all the time."

DECIDE YOU WANT TO MANAGE YOUR ATTITUDE

You probably have already decided to control your perspective on things or you wouldn't be reading this book. Good for you. Right there, that sets you apart from the kazillion people who don't know to or know how to manage their attitudes. Let's take Saturdays for example. Most everyone looks forward to Saturdays. You've seldom heard people talk about a "blue Saturday" the way they dread a "blue Monday." But is Saturday any different from any other day? The sun comes up and it goes down. There is good and there is bad weather. There is the same number of hours as any other day of the week. Yet most everyone likes Saturday better than Monday. The only difference is you typically work on Monday and you have Saturday off. The day doesn't change. Your *attitude* toward the day changes.

When you were first informed about getting your current job, wasn't that a great day? Weren't you thrilled? Wasn't it fun telling your friends and family? Of course it was. But you forget as monotony sets in. But what's really happening? Has the job changed? Is it truly boring, tedious work, or do you just view it as that because you can do it with your eyes closed? For today—no, for this *week*— I want you to thank the gods for the *fun* job you have. Whenever a minor (or major) irritation occurs, stop and look for something good about it. Then remind yourself as often as necessary until you've altered your outlook and regained your original enthusiastic attitude.

Now what do you think would happen if you anticipated Monday and Tuesday and Wednesday with the same glee that you have for Saturday, or could routinely muster the same joy you felt the first day on the job? I'll tell you. You just might end up having a better Monday, Tuesday, and Wednesday! It's all in your head, as they say. It's all attitude management.

Headed home after a couple of days out of town presenting speeches, I often write on the plane. When the clouds clear and I see the land below, I think, "That looks so good." The land is southeastern Colorado—not bad, but no garden spot either. In fact, many times the landscape isn't as pretty as the scenery of the part of the country I was just in. The reason southeastern Colorado looks so beautiful is because I am *close to home*. It's the view I choose to take. Garrison Keillor wrote, "Sometimes you need to look reality in the eye, and deny it." In other words, you need to talk to yourself the way *you need* to talk to yourself: positively, productively, constructively.

There is only one person in this world who can give you healthy self-esteem—*you*! Public opinion is insignificant compared to your private opinion. What you think of yourself, and what you tell yourself, are what will determine your fate. You have power over your attitude. In fact, it comes with an on/off switch! If you have doubts about yourself and communicate it either verbally or nonverbally to others or just to yourself, you can only imagine what doubts others will have! As UCLA basketball coach John Wooden says, "Do not let what you can't do interfere with what you can do." It's all attitude management and self-talk.

Self-approval requires you first to convince yourself, by developing a positive opinion of yourself, appearing positive, and acting positive. From positive thoughts come positive goals. If everyone seems to have a problem, you may truly be the one with the problem. And chances are the problem stems from poor attitude management and negative self-talk. When you think negatively and critically about others, you're practicing mental voodoo. Remember the voodoo doll dressed up like someone you don't like, and how you stick needles into it to create pain? That's what you do to yourself when you indulge in negative thoughts, except you're the doll. You can easily slip and stick yourself with your reckless needle pushing. Check out this "voodoo doll talk" from one individual: "I keep fueling my own anger. Every time I think about past and present injustices in my life, I get mad again and start screaming inside. I feel trapped."

If you change your mind—change your self-talk, you can have success in 30 seconds, as proven by this letter I received from Attorney Lawrence Land of Norfolk, Virginia.

All of us have a very strong positive self-image and a very strong negative self-image. We constantly inhibit ourselves from succeeding with daily tasks because of our fear of rejection and/or failure. We have a good idea what will improve our standing or the world situation. We immediately begin to think that someone has already thought of this same idea and therefore we refuse to act on it. I am convinced if we think of an idea, we need to convert our thoughts into actions within 30 seconds from the time we think of it. You should record your idea on a tape recorder, write it down, type it into your computer, or make a phone call to someone you trust. We must practice obtaining small successes every day by taking immediate action within 30 seconds from the time you formulate your ideas. Your confidence will continue to grow and you will begin to have major successes which will have major impact on your life and the lives of others.

If I had not suppressed the negative thoughts of potential rejection when I first saw my future wife, I would never have the continuous happiness that I have experienced as a result of taking action within 30 seconds after seeing her across the room at a party. As a matter of fact, friends around me reinforced the fear of rejection by telling me that there was no way I would have a chance because she was so beautiful and there were five men waiting to meet her. Within 30 seconds, I was able to meet her and begin our wonderful life together. If I had listened to my friends and listened to my inner negative self, my life would be entirely different today. More recently, I thought of an idea for the Lexus car. I wrote to the president immediately after thinking of the idea, hoping that he would improve upon the new series. Within six months, I received a call from the public relations department of the president of Lexus telling me that they wanted to use my idea and needed my permission to do so. I was ecstatic to think that they would incorporate my idea. As payment whenever I travel to any city in the country, I call the Lexus dealership in advance and they provide a new car for me to use.

Another client provides this useful analogy regarding the self-talk issue.

At work my emotions run up and down like a roller coaster, but it's important I set a good example for my people. Sometimes I catch myself 20 times a day having to rein in my attitude. I try to remember my attitude is like driving a car: I need to stay in my lane with good driving. If I start to swerve toward the ditch, I correct my steering. If I start to cross over into another lane, I correct my steering. The same is true for my attitude. If it starts going "into the ditch" or "swerving" off the road, I change it. Managing my attitude that way helps me maintain my sanity and I think people notice in a good way.

Joseph Costello, formerly CEO of Cadence Design Systems and now chairman of Cad.Lab, has as part of his personal philosophy to "begin things with a positive end in mind." It's not an overdone, sugarcoated, syrupy-positive perspective but one of good sense and good nature. It's giving yourself personal respect, like you give others. You don't have to be a perfect employee, perfect manager, perfect spouse, perfect parent, perfect child; you just need to feel adequate.

Obviously, I am not denying the reality of a "neurological El Niño" as Michael Riley of the *Home News Tribune* puts it. Everyone feels weird sometimes, like actor Peter Fonda, who recalls, "I always thought of myself as being cut loose into this weird world with my sister, and no instruction book." Nevertheless, your first assignment is to accept the idea of being adequate.

YOU'RE ADEQUATE, REGARDLESS OF EVERYTHING

Why should your self-talk mantra be "I'm adequate?" It doesn't sound high enough does it? It is. After you achieve adequacy, you can go for super-fantastic. But today, be happy with adequate. There are many in the world who would like you to feel inadequate, especially in the psychiatric/therapy world. In 1952 there were 60 listings in *The Diagnostic and Statistical Manual of Mental Disorders*. That latest version contains 145, more then double!

If you ask, "How can I be positive when I feel so out of sorts?" Well, you need to get yourself checked out medically. According to Eli Lilly and Co. (the manufacturer of the antidepressant Prozac), between 15 million and 20 million people are clinically depressed, but nearly two-thirds of those people go untreated. Some depression is real. Some is imagined. As an example, CNN reported on a study that showed 40 percent of the people studied got depressed *thinking* they had Lyme disease when they didn't.

If nothing is wrong healthwise, to get out of your funk, you need to change your perspective, manage your attitude, and control your self-talk. Have you ever been guilty of being quick tempered, anxious, worried about public speaking, preferring isolation to a group, eccentric dress, being unable to make small talk, a deadbeat anything, unhappiness about how you look, overprotectiveness, repetitive behavior that interferes with daily life, road rage, constant handwashing, keeping a superneat desk, mood swings, holding grudges, spending too much time on the Internet? Well, you get the idea; we're all in the same boat. We're all crazy in some way. I'm the most sane person I know and I'm a little weird sometimes! It's not some disorder that causes this, but free will. Labeling or compartmentalizing is an excuse.

Today, you can blame *newly documented,* biologically-based mental illnesses as the cause of shyness, intermittent rage disorder, the adult form of attention deficit disorder, schizotypal personality disorder (schizophrenia), antisocial personality disorder, obsessive-compulsive disorder, and other brain abnormalities I can't even spell. It's most interesting that we blame neurobiology for our negative behavior: e.g., "My alcoholism caused me to hit on the secretary." But we *don't* blame genes for the good things that we are proud of: courage, kindness, intelligence, hard work, and the like. What we like about ourselves becomes self-image. What we dislike we call disease.

Biology is not destiny. Only in extreme cases are people unable to willfully activate healthy thoughts to dominate unhealthy ones. Your brain creates patterns based on your thoughts, and your mind is what this chapter is all about—your mental energy. The world decathlon record holder, Dan O'Brien, has attention deficit disorder (ADD). Still he says, "Parents shouldn't use ADD as an excuse for every kid who doesn't want to study. Shut the TV off and give the kid some attention." O'Brien was given up at birth by his Finnish mother and African-American father and spent two years in foster homes before being adopted by a white couple. He's chosen to take the attitude, "A winner always finds a way."

If people can't blame biology, they blame their childhood. I have zero sympathy for people who say, "I'm the way I am because of my upbringing." WRONG. Even Truman Capote (who was somewhat strange as an adult) wrote, "One cannot go on being a damaged child forever." It's like the bumper sticker you see, "It's never too late to have a happy childhood." If you're less than adequate at something, you're the way you are because you want to be and are too lazy to change. Why am I so harsh? Because I've seen hundreds of people who've had less than ideal upbringings live stellar lives. One friend in particular comes to mind.

Out of respect for her and in the name of "political correctness," I will skip many of the details of what was done to her. It's history. As a five-year-old my friend and her family were captured and placed in a concentration camp. The teachers from the private school she attended were buried alive in a pit in front of her and the other children. She herself had her tongue slit across several times so she couldn't eat, and her fingernails were pulled out at the roots. Then her mother was decapitated in front of her on the town square. You still want to talk tough upbringing? This all happened. Yet today, this woman is one of the most memorable, impressive, credible, trusted, liked, fun people I know. In most cases, nothing can cause you damage except yourself.

For a mentally happy life, you have to disregard your past. Disregard does not mean diminish, deny, or forget. It means regardless of the past, you are a thinking adult. Your life is yours to choose to live, think, and behave the way you want.

TALK TO YOURSELF THE WAY YOU WANT OTHERS TO TALK ABOUT YOU

Don't say things to yourself that you wouldn't want said about you. Thinking and saying good things to yourself doesn't make them immediately true, but it makes for a happier life in the meantime. It's funny how we value others' opinions over our own. But as I've said, public opinion takes a backseat to your private opinion. What you think of yourself is what determines your fate.

The impossible becomes possible because you believe it. If a CEO can get people to believe something like, "We provide the highest quality service in North American," it can happen. This approach to goal achievement works on a personal as well as a corporate level. Sam Sanderson, CEO of Savvis Communication, says, "I had two big dreams in the last 10 years, two crisp, simple goals. The first dream was to be the president of a company. Within four years and nine months of setting the goal, I had the job. The second dream was to become CEO by the time I was 50 years old. Six months and fourteen days before my 50th birthday, I became CEO."

Dan O'Brien talks to himself during a race. "I think, 'Quick, quick, quick! Boom, boom, boom!' It helps," he says. Self-talk can be directed to get you to think about your potential, not your limitations, the self you want to be and the self you want others to see. When you are growing up, adults tell you you can be anybody and do anything you want. Yet we forget it. If it is true for a youngster, it's true for an oldster. It's a great gift to give yourself: to live with awareness of the power of your mind.

Says Dr. Robert Hahn, epidemiologist with the Center for Disease Control in Atlanta, "Your state of mind can even be fatal. For example, surgical patients die on the operating table because they expect to die. If you think you'll get well, you're much more likely to recover." And this is reinforced by one of the world's most celebrated brain surgeons, Dr. Benjamin Carson: "People need hope. The mind controls so much of the body. We are much more than flesh and blood; we are complex systems. Patients do better when they have faith that they're going to do better." Don't just make a difference in your day, make a difference in your life.

My husband and I were camping a hundred miles from the nearest town in one of the remotest parts of Colorado (not a city, a town of about 1500 people). A cowboy was herding some stray calves in a high pasture. He rode up to us and we introduced ourselves and started talking. Turns out we had a mutual friend in my hometown and that got him started. Somehow the conversation turned to my coaching work, and this 68-year-old cowboy surprised me with, "You know, my wife and I rent movie videos every weekend. My favorites are motivational speakers. I like to see the stories where you can dream and be anything you want." This from a cowboy on a horse in the middle of the mountains!

CATCH YOUR SELF-TALK 100 TIMES A DAY IF NECESSARY *AND* CORRECT YOURSELF

If you choose to live the way I'm writing about in this book, *do it all the time,* not just when you're relaxed, feel comfortable, people around you are pleasant, and the stars are in the right position. Do it always and everywhere. Amen. Consistency is the key. Inconsistency appears fake, unnecessarily strenuous, and gutless. Slipups that are corrected consistently are forgiven, and respect is given for the effort. Slipups uncorrected, even occasionally, really get noticed.

You don't learn from the lack of self-discipline. You set a lousy example to co-workers (and your children). You take away from the times you stand to be in control. There cannot be a gap between what you should do and what you actually do. If you let even one little boo-boo slip in and go uncorrected, you've lost. Be happy when you catch yourself doing something wrong. That means you're paying attention. And I can assure you, if you pay attention to what you're doing—all of the time, others will pay attention too. Too often, people think of what I'm preaching as something to do only in the presence of their bosses. Wrong. Do the right thing with the taxi driver, the waitress, the most junior co-worker you encounter today, and the most senior co-worker you encounter today. If you catch yourself 100 times today, maybe you'll only have to catch yourself 99 times tomorrow and 98 the next day.

The reason consistency is so important is that it creates patterns. Patterns are what people respond to—and what they remember. That's what your "reputation" amounts to, the patterns you establish. The advantage of establishing positive patterns is that if you do occasionally mess up, unintentionally and unknowingly, you'll be forgiven sooner.

DO THE OPPOSITE

If you think about what I've said so far regarding mental energy, it boils down to *doing the opposite* of what you'd normally do and what others typically do. When you try something, if it does not generate the reaction or response you want, then quickly change your tactics. Do something completely different. Go for the opposite of what you were doing. If that still doesn't work, try something else radically different.

Super Bowl quarterback Joe Montana explains how to hold a football in the rain: "Your instinct is to tighten your grip. But you need to loosen it. A wet ball is like greased lightning. The harder you squeeze it, the rougher it is to throw." Doing the opposite of expectation is what mind control is all about. It seems human nature is to be negative. I want you to be positive, or at least neutral. I want your thoughts toward work, other people, and life to be productive and constructive, not destructive.

There is a clothing store I like in LaJolla, California. Every time I go in, I find the "perfect" thing and I buy it. It is as if the owner looked into my closet, saw what was missing, and is providing it. Despite the amount of business I've given this shop, the clerks are *never* friendly toward me. It is almost like I'm bothering them and interrupting their routine when I make a purchase. So one day, to the rudest of the group, I gave a deck of cards.[1] A little surprised by the gesture, she thanked me. The next time I went in, she and the other clerks were very friendly. The owner came over and gave me an item she thought I'd like. The next time I visited, the same thing happened! By doing the opposite of what most people would do (and what I felt like doing), the situation completely turned around.

Doing the opposite gives you nice surprises, plus it makes you more creative, disciplined, innovative, and knowledgeable. Diana Vreeland, late editor of *Vogue,* used to say, "Always give ideas away. Because under every idea there is another waiting to be born." She did the opposite and was creative too. Doing the opposite makes for good humor. I particularly liked one Wrangler advertisement that featured six-time World Champion All-Around Cowboy Ty Murray high on a bull. The accompanying ad copy read, "Our jeans have rivets that don't scratch. Bulls are mad enough already." So while you give yourself a pat on the back for catching yourself 100 times a day—so you'll improve, catch others trying to improve and acknowledge them as well.

I want you to be so effective that you can forget about your own effectiveness and concentrate on helping others be more so. That's doing the opposite of what most people do: helping maintain the self-esteem of others (discussed more in Chapter 6). That's being memorable, impressive, credible, genuine, trusted, and liked. I was in San Francisco and happened to walk the same route three days in a row. The same panhandler was on the same corner, three days in a row. I never gave him money, but I did smile and say "hello" every time (like I would if he was an important client). The fourth day he saw me coming. He straightened up his posture, stuck his paper cup out, shook it so the coins would rattle, and said, "I have enough money to buy you a drink. Could I?" For the record, I did not take him up on the offer, but look at the victory for self-esteem, his, simply by treating a so-called down-and-outer the way you'd treat anyone else. Do the opposite of what most people would do:

- Control negative thoughts.
- Give yourself consistent, good, self-talk.
- Feel adequate always.

Pay attention to your mind first, before your body. The mind shows its shape through the body. But now let's give some time to talking about the body, your physical presence, the physical energy level. This will lead us to the work in Chapter 5.

Questions to ask yourself

- Do I want to manage my attitude?
- Do I see the value and importance of doing that?
- Can I fathom only holding positive, productive, or constructive thoughts?
- Will I cease self-doubting thoughts and negative self-talk?

The answer should be "yes" to all of the above.

Tools to fit the job at hand

- Your mantra: "I'm adequate."
- Talking to yourself the way you want others to talk to you.
- Catching (and correcting) yourself 100 times a day.
- Doing the opposite of what most people do and what you'd typically do.

The variety of targets possible

- Handling the inevitable negative work, people, and life situations that can take away so much of the fun and productivity.
- Controlling attitudes instead of them controlling you.
- Avoiding emotional flashing or wearing emotions on your sleeve (letting your mood come right to the surface).
- Looking for perspectives other than your own.
- Learning to "suffer fools" (so you don't look like one yourself).
- Being justifiably likable over time as well as being instantly likable.
- Showing compassion, not a cold and prickly attitude.

Strategy to go forward: Dealing With Negative People

- It's best to deal with negative issues the first time you see them and not wait until they become habitual.
- Change your attitude about the person (or the situation); cease thinking the negative.
- Take a piece of paper and write down at least three "good" things about the "negative" person.
- Every time you have to deal with the person, repeat the three things over and over in your head.

- For every negative the person comes up with, without sounding tit-for-tat, respond with a positive, productive, constructive perspective on the same issue.

- Use the "feel-felt-found" formula to discuss issues with the person. For example,

  "I think I understand how you *feel* about _____.

  Others have *felt* the same until they *found* _____.

  It acknowledges their concern and identifies the fact that others have felt similarly until presented with new thinking.

- Keep at this consistently with this person.

- Be firm but pleasant. Be relaxed in tone of voice and facial expression.

- Give *positive* people the same equitable treatment you give the *negative* ones.

- Rehearse all of the above prior to your next encounter with the individual(s).

- Don't put the person down. Rather, set an example of how you will deal with issues in a productive, constructive manner only.

- Tell the person clearly what and how you want things done. Give succinct direction, then end the conversation—pleasantly. If someone starts a negative tirade, interrupt and redirect the conversation.

- Wrap up any discussion with a positive recap and state, "Don't you agree," like you assume he or she does. (But don't get into debate.)

Fall-back plans

- Everybody is motivated by different things. Find out what is important to the "negative" person you're dealing with. For example, is it status, popularity, ego, desire for approval, security, pride, saving money, saving time, saving effort, avoiding pain, having pleasure?

- Also consider that the person may be acting as they are because they feel forced to from above, forced to because that's the way it's always been done, or to try to please others, or to avoid conflict or mistakes, or to avoid change.

- Ask the person's point of view.

- If you want to be effective with negative people, deal with them the way *they need* to be dealt with.

- Don't allow a negative style to dictate, compromise, dominate, or dilute the way you've determined is best for you.

- You can ignore some negativity. Sometimes a person does it just to "get at" you because she or he knows you don't buy into it.

NOTE

1. My aunt works for a Las Vegas casino and has contacts who provide me the "real" cards used at the gaming tables. I always carry some around to give to people.

USING PHYSICAL ENERGY: PERCEPTION MANAGEMENT

A study has shown that at any given moment, there are 40,000 people in the U.S. who don't realize they are walking around with their flies open. One's best intentions and one's behavior aren't always in sync. You need to make sure that doesn't happen to you—literally and figuratively.

This chapter's focus is on "attitude" of the body: your standing posture, style in motion, verbal delivery. The goal here is to achieve the appearance of being completely unfazed, thoroughly relaxed and at ease, relaxed—but alert—both in mind and body. This chapter is not about empty showmanship but on creating an authentic appearance that is memorable, impressive, credible, genuine, trusted, and liked.

Although attitude is tough to maintain, it *can* be hidden. But behavior and physical actions *can't* be hidden as easily. People you meet will size you up in about eight seconds flat, and they draw their conclusions based on what they see. To make life easier and to be sized up in the manner you want to be, your attitude must support your actions and vice versa. It's simple perception management in an image-driven world.

Perception management takes work. Remind yourself that anything worth striving for requires effort, commitment, and tenacity over the long term. No matter how far back you slip or how hard you fall down, get up and don't give up. It's that simple. As the saying goes, "Even a continuous drop of water on cement eventually wears the cement down."

Remember the part in Chapter 4 about "catching yourself" 100 times a day? That's just the start of your coaching. Part two is, *be willing to make the big bet 14 times a day*. What do I mean by that? The "big bet" means some courageous action, something where there is risk involved, something that's a gamble. We've already established that the foundation for success is mental energy. Attitude is an elusive thing that can be easily swayed unless it is constantly checked. A lot of talking is going on inside your head at any given time that no one can see.

Physical energy, on the other hand, is largely symbolic. Symbols, or signs, are what people see and respond to. They stir pride, make a call to action, comfort, and help people relate. People don't always know the meaning of the sign, but they know it causes a positive (or negative) reaction in them. Symbolism sends messages to all involved. Sumo wrestlers take a symbolic drink of "power water" for good luck just before a match. They clap their hands to summon the spirits. Then they stomp the ground to scare the evil spirits away from the area they wrestle in. Without the symbolism, the actions, the show, it could look just like two skimpily dressed fat guys pushing each other around. Symbolic actions require *physical energy.*

On average, you need to lay your attitude on the line 14 times a day. You need to make the big bet with your behavior by choosing how you will act in each circumstance. It boils down to theatrics, like the drama and melodrama we play out every day in our personal and professional lives. The acting, the symbolism, and the staging will all be discussed at length in this chapter. You will see that *five minutes of the right "bet," or choice of behavior, is worth five years of hard work.* It boils down to efficiency and quality of motion.

TENACITY BREEDS DISCIPLINE, WHICH CREATES PATTERNS AND HABITS

Sometimes, very intelligent people can be stunningly undisciplined. None of what has been discussed in this book so far will make any difference in your life without the decision, determination, and discipline to *do it,* and not just occasionally. What you do once is one measure of skill. But what you can do *upon demand* is what counts. "Upon demand" becomes habit. Upon demand is what forms *instinct.* Your destiny is determined by your instincts. With repeated, effective actions, you hone your instincts.

No matter how well-trained you are, there's someone out there just as trained and just as driven and who would like to beat you. So you must be better in some way, and that way is discipline. It is the difference between making it or not. First is mental discipline, then physical discipline.

1. Never give up on yourself.

2. Never let up on yourself.

3. Never let yourself down.

You will surprise yourself. Keep punching away at it, making the bet, and one day you'll get lucky.

"Nobody who ever gave his best regretted it." said legendary Chicago Bears coach George Halas. Discipline does not mean speed. Too often people think discipline means hard work, and hard work means doing a lot, and doing a lot means do it fast so you'll have time to do more. The result is fruitless speed. *Slow down.*

QUIET SPEED: SLOW DOWN TO GET THINGS DONE

I was in a meeting with two department heads discussing group training for some entry-level people. In bursts a woman to inform one of the people about a change in appointments. With rapid-fire words she explained the schedule change. Then as quickly as she had come in, she was gone. I asked, "Is she one of the entry-level people I'll be working with?" They smiled and said, "No, that's who we report to!"

Boy, was I wrong! My opinion was based on her appearance, a hasty, nervous-looking person who zipped in and out with hunched over posture, saying nonverbally, "I'm not that important and I really shouldn't be here, but . . ."

Men and women up and down the ladder must slow down for efficiency. Harness your energy. One guy I know says he tries to "start out slow and taper off." The things you're getting in this book are harder to master when you're in a hurry. Slow down so you don't stumble and so you don't leave gaps.

A big advantage of going slowly is that if you're headed in the wrong direction, you won't go too far before you realize it. Slowing down does not mean squelching your spirit. It means pacing. Pace yourself so you are fast enough but not frantic, so you have a quiet speed that makes you look relaxed, calm, and trustworthy. Speed tends to make you appear unsettled, upset, flustered, confused, and suspicious. The actions of effective people do not seem rushed.

As people around you speed up, try the opposite, as we discussed in Chapter 4. A client from Hewlett-Packard told me this story:

I always speak fast—on the telephone, in person, giving speeches—all the time. But I was in Germany recently and had to speak to a group through an interpreter. After every sentence I spoke, I had to pause and let the translator restate what I said. I was slower than I had ever been in my life. It made me very calm. My English-speaking manager came up to me later and said it was the best speech he'd ever heard me present. Many people in the audience came up and congratulated me also. Now when I speak, I just imagine someone is translating my words into their language and I slow down to let them catch up. I've found I'm much more effective.

A lot of people believe the busier they are the better they are. But if you want to be memorable, impressive, credible, genuine, trusted, and liked, don't "run around the track" for anybody.

To get things done more quickly while slowing down, ask yourself, "If I had to leave town tomorrow for a month, what three things would I need to get done?" Do those three things. "Controlled reaction thinking" is the goal. Slow down your body, feet, and hands. Quick thinking is necessary, but *pace* your physical response. For practice, do a silent drill. Rehearse in your head what you're going to say. Listen to how it sounds. Then speak accordingly. Slow down, let people wait a little. Whatever you say or do will be valued that much more. By the way, this is incredibly difficult to do. We just blurt things out 90+ percent of the time. I try to do this silent drill at least once a day. If I don't accomplish it—in a totally deliberate way, I force myself to do it twice the next day.

You don't want to be viewed like one client, who was sent to me with this description: "He thinks he's so thoroughly trained he doesn't have to think before he speaks and acts. I can't trust him, he's so fast." Slowing down does not mean you're boring, listless, tedious, or lazy. It means doing things purposefully, like you intended to do it that way. It means patience, then acceleration, then patience. You see, 95 percent of business is waiting, waiting for the opportunity to do the right thing. If you're going through life so fast, you'll miss the chance to execute one of those incredible strokes that gets five years of work done in five minutes.

When you slow down, you buy yourself time and you can think things through. And when you think things through, you can give yourself the time of your life. When you slow down and *think,* you align attitude and action, and you appear calm and confident. You'll feel more composed too. When you appear calm, people think you know what you're doing. They think you must be right. They are much more likely to listen and follow you. When you have a relaxed manner, you get your best results, whether you are a runner, boxer, rodeo rider, or businessperson. As comedienne Lily Tomlin puts it, "For fast-acting relief, try slowing down."

ACTIONS FIT YOUR ATTITUDE AND CREATE YOUR FIRST IMPRESSION

In a recent conversation with the female operating head of a *Fortune* 200 company, she told me, "After months of working on all we talked about, Debra, I've concluded success is all about two things: (1) how I view myself, and (2) how others view me."

Your first impression has a profound influence on all the future estimation and opinion people will hold of you. So be careful. The future can last a long time. Even renowned Harvard economist John Kenneth Galbraith addressed this aspect of business: "People working together in the corporation are motivated overwhelmingly by their desire to have the good opinion of their colleagues. Without this the modern corporation would be a failure."

Moreover, a recent Harvard study concluded that you *should* trust your first impression of others; it's probably right. Psychologists showed a group of students three- to five-second videotaped clips of professors teaching. The students were asked to rate the professors' effectiveness based on those few seconds of observation. Their ratings turned out virtually identical to the ratings the teachers received from students who had taken classes with them for an entire semester.

Your first impression is like looking in a mirror—it's right there. What people see is what people think they are getting. I'm sorry to be the bearer of this news, but in business life, you have to watch every single nuance. As Dan Jansen, an Olympic gold medal winner, explains, "You can't win on your first day (of racing), but you can lose." The same is true of your first impression. To create an effective first impression, from your opening act on, *act!*

You can still be the genuine thing even though you are acting. Act out your attitudes. This creates your first impression. See why it is so important that your attitude is productive, constructive, and positive? People are going to see! Accept the fact that sometimes you have to perform symbolic gestures.

Edward Crutchfield, CEO of First Union Corporation, is a big, charismatic fellow who wants his employees to know he runs a "people place." He regularly meets with small groups who've never met him. He undoes his necktie as he initiates his icebreaker "opening act." With a humorous tone in his voice, he says, "I bet no one here has the guts to ask me an insulting question." To prove his sincerity in being interested in his employees' needs, he wraps up the session by giving them his home phone number.

Then there's the story handed down about Henry Kissinger. It came from John Love, who was enery czar during the Reagan years and who hails from my home state of Colorado. It seems Love had the opportunity to meet with Kissinger and during the discussion, he asked Kissinger how he approached solving the complicated problems he had such a reputation for tackling. What was his methodology, the research, the analysis for dealing with the complex issues, Love asked. Kissinger slowly responded in his thick accent, "Well, the first thing I do is make the problem *look* difficult."

Bob Crutchfield and Kissinger understand the requirement for theatrics on the job. Theatrics is *not* artifice. It is accepting the responsibility to give people you are dealing with the picture you want them to see and therefore perceive. If you don't do it, because it seems fake, you're 100 percent wrong! I want to pause here to reiterate an assumption I am making. You, the reader, are a hard-working, results-oriented, high-integrity, ambitious, goal-oriented individual who wants to be memorable, genuine, and all the rest. You have everything the corporate world needs more of. But you don't always get the credit you're due, the recognition and reward, or even the simple expression of appreciation. So *you* have to do something about that. That is why you're acting on the need to coach yourself, to better ensure this is all going to happen. It takes some acting. The fact is, we all have good times and bad times, good days and bad days. To get through them takes acting.

Top executives in business learn to display emotional drama to appear confident, positive, and upbeat, even when they aren't. Leaders can't slump, scowl, stare, or otherwise look uncomfortable in front of colleagues, employees, customers, or the competition. Business leaders don't have the option of looking how they really feel. And neither do you. People watch their leaders and decide if they are up, down, or sideways. Typically, it is wise to maintain the impression that everything is under control. That takes acting.

A friend of mine, Katherine Cizynski, Vice President at James Mead & Company, told me, "As an executive recruiter, I am expected to instill confidence in individuals who have placed their careers in my hands. It is essential that I not only provide them substantive feedback but that I do so in a highly professional manner.

At one time, eager to listen, with a frequent bobbing of my head, I now take a more subdued approach characterized by an occasional head gesture or words that indicate my desire to hear more. I appear relaxed, comfortable, and in control."

When a person "performs" in a business situation, it may take the form of something like:

- Giving an understanding nod—when you don't fully understand.
- Listening with rapt attention—when you really aren't that interested.
- Laughing at the right time—not because what was said was so funny, but because you know it's expected.
- Smiling knowingly—when you're truly hoping you just don't get found out!
- Making the rounds saying hello—not because you want to meet or talk with everyone but because you are supposed to.
- Struggling with yawns—in class, in church, in a board meeting, on a date.
- Remaining impassive—when you're mad as hell and don't want to take it anymore.

I'm flatly recommending you should act happy, act calm, act confident, act enthusiastic, act energetic, act in control, act adequate, act pleasant, *act*, period!

Some "professionals" might say that it is "unprofessional" to give such advice, that you could mess up your mind if you act a certain way when you don't really feel it. I'm not promoting acting as a falsehood or lie, but as it's defined in the dictionary: *a short performance, to behave, to function, to have an effect on, to appear to be.* No one is always happy, calm, confident, enthusiastic, energetic, in control, adequate, and pleasant, but what kind of a miserable place would we be living in if we always showed what we really feel? Unhappy, nervous, scared, bored, lazy, out of control, inadequate, and nasty, that's what!

The odd thing about human nature is we act like it's okay to behave in those negative, destructive ways "if we feel like it." How irresponsible! I want you to do just the opposite; be positive, even if you have to act it. It won't kill you.

Here's what you need for superb acting. To start, you have to have a superb cast. (You have that—yourself!) Self-talk is used in rehearsing your script. Next, accept the fact that it's always opening night. And remember what Shakespeare wrote, "One man in his time plays many parts." All the world's a stage, and you're both player *and* director.

Fear not, you will never come across as a fraud, misfit, or nincompoop when trying to act unless you act falsely, pretending to have poise, professionalism, and worth to your organization when you don't really believe it. Nor does acting mean acting up or acting out, for example,

- Yelling or swearing at people who are doing nothing to you except being there.
- Growing your turf by taking it from others.
- Looking preoccupied and grouchy to make people nervous or uncomfortable around you.
- Cutting into a line when you don't want to wait your turn like others.
- Plastic surgery for a granite jawbone or liposuction for abs like Fabio.

Behaviors like these fall somewhere between rudeness and artifice. They are not acting in the sense I'm promoting. Made-up, manufactured, and counterfeit is bad style. Still, good style requires some acting. Try doing some simple things with a little showmanship, like:

- Remaining standing in the reception room so when you meet whoever's coming to get you, you are eye-to-eye (figuratively and literally).

- Complimenting a person in the elevator whom you've never met.

- Being the first to make small talk to your airplane seatmate.

- Carrying yourself like you are fit, even if you haven't worked out in a year.

- Dressing neatly, with attention to detail, even if you got your wardrobe at a thrift store.

- Engaging strangers in conversation at a social gathering, so they can feel more relaxed.

- Acting like you are having a good time—always. (You just might end up having one.)

Does this look like I'm asking for wild, crazy, unbelievable behavior? Just try going against the grain of what most people do and what you'd typically do.

Here's Paul Schlossberg, president of D/FW Consulting (food-service experts), on the subject of "acting" in a business context:

> *In building my consulting business public speaking became a great opportunity for me to expose my thinking process to potential clients. As I planned my speaking strategy, it occurred to me that there were several discrete elements to consider. This included content, physical delivery, challenging the audience, and being dramatic.*

First was content. My strategy was that each presentation would be unique and original. While some points might carry through, especially market-based observations or facts, the main theme would be original each time. This approach has been successful, since return invitations have been extended.

Next was physical delivery. After staying behind the podium, I learned to wander around. New tools were required. A lavaliere microphone. A remote slide control for my computer. These tools turned out to be very effective.

Next was to challenge the audience. This involved being a bit controversial. My focus was to deny commonly accepted norms. To tell the audience that in some cases radically different behavior would be necessary to change the status quo . . . making them feel a bit uncomfortable. The personal impact of being relaxed and up close and personal made my challenges more acceptable.

Finally, I decided to be dramatic. Why enter from "stage left" when you can walk in from the back (from the last row of the audience)? This was a bit startling and captured attention quickly. The ability to talk with individuals one-to-one, almost face-to face, while giving the talk is a powerful speaking technique.

The real payoff is that about 75 percent of my speaking "dates" resulted in a connection to develop a client relationship.

Regularly thinking about new ways to be dramatic and work on physical delivery forced me to be much more creative and bold in making presentations.

Some interesting things you'll learn about the benefits of acting as an element in your self-coaching:

- If you act calm, you'll end up feeling more calm.
- If you act confident, people treat you as if you are, and you become more confident.
- If you act energetic, you'll get energized.

You pretty much become how you behave, so you may as well choose actions that are productive and constructive.

The only job security you can reasonably expect comes from being more talented and skilled tomorrow than you are today. You will have a richer life if you put forth the effort, and, of course, this entails deciding you are worth the effort. I think you are. But what actions should you start with? The ones you do daily.

THE MINUTIAE OF ACTING: CHECK YOUR POSTURE, WALK, AND SMILE

Know what you're looking for. Observe, then imitate. It's never too late to pick a role model—someone you want to sit, walk, and stand like. Boxer George Foreman picked John Wayne. As Foreman says, "Sometimes he (Wayne) wasn't taller than the other guys in the movies, but he sat, stood, and walked as if he was."

During college I spent a vacation week in Spain. One day I saw a woman walk up the street and enter the sidewalk cafe where I was eating. She stood in the entrance waiting for her lunch partner. She had impeccable carriage, a pleasant expression, and executed a grand but tasteful gesture as she removed her turquoise gloves, which matched her turquoise pants suit, purse, and shoes. It was 1973 when I saw this woman, yet today I can see her as clearly in my head as if it were yesterday. For some reason she was the epitome of grace and confidence to me. Probably 1000 times since the day I saw her, I've brought her back into my mind as a personal example.

Stand Tall

A recent *Vanity Fair* cover shot by Fran Lebowitz showed Arnold Schwarzenegger standing on top of a mountain in a white T-shirt—with great posture. The photo was taken after his heart surgery and after he turned 50 years old, but he could surely be the poster-boy for good posture.

Feel proud. Stand proud. There is *nothing* wrong with that. It perplexes me to no end that so few people do. Poor posture comes from laziness, modesty, or maybe lack of a good example. My mother has excellent posture and carriage. I remember watching her walk up the church aisle one Sunday, and I overheard Sister Agnes say, "That Benton woman walks too proud." It struck me as so odd, because a split second before the good Sister's comment, I was watching my mother and thinking, "Wow, does she look good. I like the way she walks."

My good Catholic upbringing taught me excellent ethics, along with the less-than-perfect lesson "don't be proud." Many religions glorify modesty and teach the-meek-inherit-the-earth lessons. Then we mistakenly carry that into our posture, which affects our attitude. I prefer to think that pose suggests dignity and that God wants us dignified. Disregard public pressure to succumb to the loser slouch. People will notice and appreciate you so much more. Keep your head straight, not tilted downward, upward, or to the side, and look straight ahead. Keep your neck straight, with your shoulders evenly lowered. Keep your spine straight. Feel your body from the nape of your neck down to your toes. Lift your rib cage off your pelvis if it has sunk that low. Tuck in your rear if necessary, and your stomach as well. Take a deep breath through your nose, fill your diaphragm, pause, then exhale and say the word "relax." You want fluidity, not fixedness.

When I interviewed for my first "career" job after college, I borrowed a friend's Corvette and wore my new pink polyester dress and white shoes. The executive secretary to the man who hired me said (with good humor), "The only thing you did right was walk in with good posture." One partner at McKinsey & Company told me simply, "It's about how you walk onto the court. You need to display confidence just short of arrogance." One of the 14 "big bets," or risks, you can resolve to undertake today is when you are walking down the hallway—with good posture, ten feet from the next new person you encounter, smile; and at three feet, say "hello." In between the ten-foot and three-foot marks rehearse in your mind anything you might want to say. Watch the reaction to your "presence."

I once found myself in the ladies room of a hotel in Rancho Mirage with former First Lady Betty Ford. We were both at the mirror adjusting hair and lipstick. I thought to myself, "I'd like to say something to her but not like everybody else says, 'Oh, Mrs. Ford, so pleased to meet you.' " So I calmly inquired while looking in the mirror, "Do you suppose men primp for us like this?" And she answered, "No, with men you just take them as they come." We both smiled, finished, and left. Nothing more came of it except for the good feeling that I had in taking a few seconds to think through a comment in my head, having the courage to say it, enjoying a pleasant exchange, and ending up with a nice little story to tell you. I don't mind telling you, I walked out of there with extra-confident posture.

Walk Tall

Keep a purposeful pace—not hurried and harried—head level, toes pointed forward, arms swinging loosely, but not sloppily, free to gesture if appropriate. If you walk like a winner, you may become one. Watch Arnold Schwarzenegger walk. That's good posture. You walk into a meeting room with that carriage and people are going to notice. They will also notice if you walk into the room hunched over like a question mark, but for the wrong reasons.

Use a winning posture, at home with the kids, in a fast-food restaurant, at the beach. (In fact, I recommend a trip to Hawaii because you'll wear fewer clothes there, and if you don't hold your shoulders back, lift your rib cage off your hips, and suck in your gut, you'll look really, really bad.) Try this at the office as well—though you may want to leave the swimsuit at home. Good posture comes from muscles and discipline. A lifted sternum, for example, tends to make people smile by helping the face to relax.

Put on a Happy Face

Above all, smile. By "smile," I mean maintain an affable countenance that makes you look good-natured, friendly, younger, cheerful, more attractive, and gives you a kind of grace. Your business face accounts for 80 percent of your effectiveness. It adds to your "book value." Now you may say, "I don't *feel* good-natured, friendly, young, cheerful, or attractive." Then go back to Chapter 4 and start all over. You need an attitude adjustment.

Act confidently; then work on being confident. To do that, always look like you are having fun. Your face does that for you, if you hold it purposefully. Relax your jaw, lift your cheeks, open your lips, turn the corners of your mouth upward, engage with steady eyes. Keep this look on your face all day, everyday, until you die! Don't wrinkle your forehead, furrow your brow, and create "cleavage on your forehead," as comedienne Brett Butler describes it. There, you have a relaxed smile; a serene expression (whether you feel it or not). Caution: Your facial expression must never become a smirk, sneer, grimace, or leer—never, regardless of how you feel.

Since people read you like a book, it's wise to cultivate and display amiable feelings, even if it requires acting. It's easier to control your words than your countenance, but you can also control your countenance, with hard work. Your thoughts can chisel your features. I did some consulting with a number of executives at

Nabisco. One of the messages I tried to convey was the power of facial expression. I suggested if they said the word "easycheese" and kept their mouths in that position, they would have the expression I proposed: a relaxed, awake, alert look that appears competent and comfortable. (It's the look President Clinton and newscaster Dan Rather both have almost all of the time. It turns out they use the "easycheese" technique, too.) In follow-up conversations after our time together some of the participants reported on the effect. Eric Fritz said,

> The simple idea like "easycheese" has worked exceedingly well. People . . . have begun to feel more confidence in me as a person in just two to three weeks. You've made me aware of the connection between the face, heart, and brain. The value is reflecting in my face the sincere delight I feel in my heart and brain. It causes me to engage myself in positive thinking by . . . using face muscles. It's pretty cool. I was in a horrendous traffic jam in southern New Jersey yesterday. I really appreciated the simplicity and value of putting "easycheese" on. It didn't change traffic, but I felt better.

Another person in the group, John Kennington, said, "I've used this expression in keeping my spirits up during a difficult transition in the company. A lot of key decisions, most of them difficult, affecting the careers of many people, had to be made. 'Easycheese' became our mantra and kept our people focused on what they need to get done versus what would have happened in the rumor mill otherwise. My wife's been telling me for years to put on an expression like this."

No one making under $100,000 a year can afford to be surly—nor can anyone making more! The only time to take a relaxed smile off your face is when you are in the shower. That's to avoid getting soap in your mouth. Otherwise—it's your duty to keep it on.

I discovered the affect of being aware of my facial expression at an early age and have continued to use it for every situation I find myself in today. When I was 13 years old, a gangly self-conscious teen, I was walking by a construction site. Seeing all the workers and being very self-conscious, I apparently had a particularly serious look on my face. One of the workers yelled out, "Little lady, it takes fewer muscles to smile than frown, and you'll look a whole lot happier." Although I remembered his coaching, I didn't receive it well at the time. I flashed him a disdainful look, thinking, "Who does he think he is talking to me that way?"

But as I say, I remembered it and practiced it and found he was right. That evening, I was going to a movie with my father. As a teen it wasn't that cool going with a parent. The "in" crowd went with friends. I didn't have a date and truth was, my Dad was my best friend. Standing in the ticket line with my father, squeezed between the cools kids, I practiced some heavy-duty smiling. Now kids aren't "supposed" to look that way even if they're happy. But I opted to do the opposite, and I remember we both had the best time. I used it the next day when my parents took the family water skiing. Hanging on the back of a tow rope going 30 miles an hour on one water ski, I put on the best smile possible. Beaming through the fear resulted in less fear. In the same amount of time of being sullen, you will accomplish more by having a relaxed smile. And it is more natural. Sullen is a learned behavior. If you practice every day, all day long, you'll make it a habit—a habit of mind and body.

A number of years later in a college class, we were role-playing job interviews and being videotaped. As young graduates ready to conquer the world, we were quite impressed with ourselves. I thought I'd experiment and do half of my taped practice interview with my serious student look and half with a relaxed smile (even though I did not feel like smiling). I was too embarrassed to tell anyone what I was doing, thinking it might appear foolish. But I was absolutely shocked when I replayed the tape. I wouldn't have hired the person in the first half of the tape, but I sure would have hired the person in the second half.

I decided to take it further. A group of my female friends would go to the local clubs in hopes of meeting guys. We had this "tradition" that the first one to get asked to dance had all her food and beverage expenses paid for the evening by the other girlfriends. Being fairly competitive and usually low on money, I wanted to win. So I practiced smiling. I smiled when sitting. I smiled when looking around or talking. I smiled when walking to the restroom. And I generally got asked to dance first, despite not being the most attractive of the group.[1]

Smiling has probably served me better in business than any other "style" technique I know. Putting on a happy, relaxed face doesn't make problems go away, but it does improve attitude. Psychologist Randy Larsen of the University of Michigan says, "Manipulating the muscles of the face into a smile enhances pleasure." The muscle movements of a smile alter the blood flow to the brain in ways that enhance your sense of well-being.

Among the other benefits of smiling are:

- Burns calories
- Gives strength
- Begets reciprocal smiles
- Helps you live longer and healthier
- Adds more than $10,000 to $20,000 of income a year (according to an informal poll)
- Generates trust
- Makes you look like you're having fun

One of the most popular Olympic skaters today is Michelle Kwan. She tells how she saw a videotape of a female skater who fell during the Olympic competition, yet got up, smiled, and continued, "That's the way I want to be," she said. The smile has to engage the face. It can't be faked with lip muscles only. The eyes have to be looking at the person you're targeting to make the rapport and connection. You don't even have to talk, just look and smile to make your connection.

Once, in the Metropolitan Museum of Art, I was sitting in a rest area when Henry Kissinger and his entourage walked by. I smiled at him, and he smiled back (sort of), more like a purposeful, deep nod of acknowledgment. That fulfilled one of my 14 big bets that day and made for another story to repeat to you. It's little victories like this that make life so much fun. You won't receive a pay raise, job promotion, or fancier title every day of your life. But you can every day give yourself one of these little "joys" in life by deliberately trying something new and experiencing a small adventure. If any question remains in your mind on why bother keeping "on" all the time, the answer is simple: Someone you are going to encounter today hasn't seen you before, and that gives you the opportunity to create the impression you want.

LOOK YOUR BEST IN YOUR BASIC APPEARANCE

Life is not fair and the most unfair part of it is that appearances count so much. Tremendous consequences come from little aspects of appearance—both good and bad consequences. You have to pay attention to details. I get way too many requests to coach people on superficial appearance: disheveled hair on both men and women, clothes like they were slept in, skirts on women or ties on men that are too short, and on and on. Economists Jeff Biddle of Michigan State University and Daniel Hamermesh of the University of Texas have studied appearance in business. They concluded that attractive workers (male and female alike) earn more than homelier colleagues. And there's other research suggesting employers may be willing to pay more for the pleasure of having an attractive person around them. A historian at West Virginia University who has written about aesthetics and the politics of hair says, "It's amazing how quickly people recognize social class in hair. There's a haircut that belongs on Wall Street and a different one that belongs in Hollywood."

I myself have waist-length gray hair. It does not fit the Wall Street or corporate model, but my husband likes it and that is paramount. In recent months two different CEOs have asked why I didn't cut and dye my hair to fit the "corporate look." To compensate a bit for this minor breach, I pull it up into a classic French twist, and I make certain every other aspect of my appearance is as "business acceptable" as possible.

Some years ago a French-based communication company, GRISBY, wanted to license my consulting programs in Europe. After lengthy negotiations, we struck a deal, part of which included my spending 10 days in France participating in their public relations tour as they kicked off the program. Fearing an American businesswoman might not know to dress suitably for the French audience, GRISBY made arrangements with the house of Christian Dior to loan me clothes for the week. I sent my sizes over in advance and they selected a wardrobe for me. They provided a loaned selection of suits and dresses and I could choose what to wear. For a Paris Press Club interview, I chose a striking black and purple dress, topped with a dramatic cape. Later, I was gently reprimanded for wearing that item before noon. Seems it was for the *afternoon.* Twenty-six reporters from the French media were there, and two of them—from the most prominent publications—chose to mention my wrong choice of clothes in their articles. Fortunately, being American, I was excused.

A vice president I know, who will remain anonymous, explained, "I'm growing a beard and am letting my hair get really long so I am undesirable to the corporate honchos. When the company is purchased, I want them to send me home with my lucrative severance package." Unfortunately, it will likely work. Make no mistake about it, people notice details. And if you aren't doing it already, you too should start paying extra attention.

I am not suggesting becoming judgmental about the appearances of others. Just be aware in general, and aware of the possible effect on others of your basic appearance. Besides, it's such an easy thing to fix. Have a conservative hairdresser and clothier help you. I say conservative because at the basic level, it's preferable to err on the side of conservative and tasteful rather than risk looking inappropriate in a premature effort at trendiness. Try to keep in mind three key points about your attire:

1. Your clothes shouldn't be more interesting than you are.

2. Apparel should fit well and appear neat and clean.

3. Choose clothes a level or two above you, or suitable to the level you want to influence.

A simple action that might save the day some time is to keep a dress or suit of clothes at the office better than you normally wear. If something important comes up that demands "dressier" clothes, you have them immediately accessible. Like women touch up their makeup during the day, if necessary, men should also keep a shaver stored in a desk drawer. How you present yourself and wear your clothes supersedes *what* you wear.

I recently received a message on my voice mail from a man who left his name but no phone number. The name sounded familiar, but I couldn't quite place it. Since he didn't leave his phone number, I couldn't call back. Fortunately, a few days later he called back. We were going over the "how's business" conversation, and he mentioned he'd seen an article in *USA Today* and wanted to see if it was the same Debra Benton. I kept racking my brain for how I knew this person. Finally, it dawned on me it might be an old client from United Airlines.

The story starts 20-plus years ago when I tried to make a sales call on three executives at United. I had started my own business and thought they would be a great client. They wouldn't see me, even after several attempts. A few weeks later I was vacationing at the Camelback Inn in Scottsdale. At that time the meeting rooms were right beside the swimming pool. I was sunning by the pool and happened to see the meeting room doors open and the three executives I'd been trying to see walked out. Now, I had a decision to make, remain on the chaise lounge and hide behind my magazine or get up, walk over, introduce myself, and ask in person to meet in their office at a convenient time. Part of the consideration was that I was wearing a swimsuit and didn't look very "professional," a *very* casual dress day, you could say! But I couldn't miss the opportunity to meet these people either. So with my best posture, carriage, and comportment, I approached them. We chatted briefly, and I asked to meet them in their office when they returned. To make a long story short, they did meet me and became one of my first clients.

Back to the phone call, when I realized the caller might be one of those men, I asked, "Did we first meet in Scottsdale?" He said, "yes," so it confirmed who I was talking to. Then I said, "You know, I was hesitant to talk with you because I wasn't dressed very appropriately." "I remember. I think they called them string bikinis at the time." he stated. As I burst out laughing, he added, "and it was blue." In hindsight my clothes might have been a tad more interesting than they should have been. Advantage or not (seriously, the impression could have gone either way), had I not taken action, the "big bet," I might never have gotten the chance to sell my business services.

THEATRICALLY SPEAKING

Your main goal has to be to make people *want* to listen, whether you are speaking one-on-one or to a group. Have something to say, say it, and stop when you've said it. Be comprehensive, but also concentrate and be succinct. Don't be so brief you are obscure, and don't hoard information. I read a survey that said women speak on average 6000 words a day; men average 2000. As a woman I'm not sure I buy that ratio, but either way, both sound like a heck of a lot! Of course, we could all afford a few less. It's okay to let others speak—a lot more than we do. Ask yourself before you say something: "Is it true, kind, or necessary?" Remember, good communication frequently involves leaving things unsaid. Still, err on the side of overcommunicating versus just communicating or undercommunicating.

Observe who gets listened to in your group, team, company, or family. Does it happen because of their language, sentence structure, words, tone of voice? What good things are they doing that you aren't and could change?

Be bold in your posture, stance, language, and volume when speaking. You may not be right, but your salesmanship may make the sale or give you a second chance. Be tentative when speaking *about* people. You may not be right, and at the least you risk looking petty or uninformed. One study shows 38 percent of your effectiveness comes from your voice. To improve yours, start by listening to the messages you leave on people's voice mail. Usually, there is an option to review it. When you review it, check to hear if the message sounds tired, stressed, harried, nervous, or filled with "umhs" and "ahs." Or does it sound upbeat, clear, succinct, measured, and worth listening to.

If the message you left doesn't sound the way you'd like it, redo it. Hopefully, the extra time and discipline necessary to do it over will teach you the lesson to do it better the next time, thus saving the need to do it twice. Spend a day this week leaving messages for people. Don't do it to meet some quota, but to apply a kind of personal *total quality management* in the message. Try these various "theatrics" when you telephone:

- Write down the key points you want to make (The listener can't see if you're referring to notes).
- Stand up when you speak.
- Have a smile on your face while dialing and keep it on.
- Breathe deeply and slowly while you are listening to the message of the person you are calling.
- If it's someone you won't be calling again, try out some "voice" you'd like to emulate. Ham it up a little!
- Speak half as fast as you normally do; throw in a dramatic pause between key points.
- Use a tone like you are talking to a person, not a computer.
- Minimize buzzwords, repetitive words, and fillers.[2]
- Interrupt if necessary; don't be overly polite if something must be corrected.

- Practice with varying inflection, volume, and pacing.
- Emphasize words, even syllables in words. (That's what David Brinkley attributes his success to.)
- Don't babble.

Your voice should sound real and truthful, with good sense and good humor.

While you're reviewing messages, listen to your own outgoing message and how it sounds to people. Don't accept the impersonalization of that computerized voice where you only add your name. Most people give their name with a voice that sounds like a prison role call. Use this checklist for your outgoing message:

1. Write your message.
2. Rehearse it with a variety of styles.
3. Record.
4. Review the recording.
5. Rerecord until you get it right.

When talking face-to-face, try talking for a half minute, then stop. Take as many half minutes as necessary. Throw in some silence. Try not to say anything anyone is going to wish had been left unsaid. Words are everything. They build trust, inspire, and show direction. They can hurt, and they can help. Words need to be picked over, weighed, combed through, and only used deliberately. When speaking or writing, be miserly with your words. Focus not on using the most words, but the right ones.

If your meaning is fuzzy, you leave room for others to operate and maneuver. Precision communication is the goal. Speaking in an indirect, roundabout way can result in miscommunication. When you're straightforward, you clearly lay out consequences. Don't speak to win points, protect your face, gain forced applause, shout down your competition, scare others, or just make noise. Remember what Larry King says, "I've never learned anything when I was talking." And keep in mind that *voice tone* is mightier than the words spoken. As one sage expressed it, "Say what you mean, mean what you say, but don't say it mean."

The marathoner, Bill Rogers, used to stride alongside a competitor and ask a planned set of questions that required more than a one word answer. He says he sized up his opponents' strength level by how timid the voice was. Then he could make his move to surge ahead. People sense (or assume) weakness or arrogance by your tone.

When you slow down, speak up, and act confidently, comfortably, and competently, people will assume you are. I'm assuming you are, but we want to make sure people *see* it. You need to get credit for being as good as you really are! If you don't, it's your fault. You need to do all you can to control your effect on others, versus leaving it to chance. Your attitude and physical energy make up two of the three required components. Chapter 6 will provide the third component, emotional energy. I want you to be one of those special people who has all three components of energy securely in your grasp.

Fortune magazine recently reported that *good* CEOs are getting harder to find. "Expectations of what a CEO should be have soared. These days, say the headhunters, people who lead large corporations need to be not only strategic thinkers with a firm handle on their industry but also charismatic, passionate leaders who bring a clear agenda the first time they walk into the boardroom. . . . Very few folks have all those attributes." Take comfort in the fact that if you hide your insecurities long enough, you may forget you have them. If you carry confidence around with you all the time, then you'll always have some when you need it.

Questions to ask yourself

- Can I accept the importance of "acting" on the job?
- Do I understand acting does not mean artifice?
- Do I appreciate the power of symbols?
- Will I tenaciously act like I should, even when I don't feel like it?
- Do I want to create new patterns and habits in my behavior?
- Am I consistently aware of when to act, and am I focusing on doing it effectively?

The answer should be "yes" to all of the above.

Tools to fit the job at hand

- Slow down. Develop a quiet speed in getting results.
- Create every effort and impression you choose to make.
- Check your posture, walk, and smile—100 times a day if necessary.
- Do what you can to be better than just "presentable" in your basic appearance.
- Speak up and speak well.
- Practice, role-play, and rehearse as much as necessary.

The variety of targets possible

- Present my ideas as well in a Group Presentation as I do one-on-one.
- Control my energy so it is productive not destructive.

- Take command (when necessary) as I walk into the room.
- Display comfortableness, competence, and confidence.
- Eliminate self-defeating mannerisms, actions, behaviors.
- Display an executive image.
- Speak up, well, and with authority.

Strategy to go forward—Making Group Presentations

- If you do well one-on-one, you can do equally well with a group—*if you remember,* "a group is made up of a bunch of one-on-ones; you're just talking to them simultaneously."
- Stop telling yourself you have difficulty giving a public presentation. Instead, tell yourself, "I'm finding it increasingly comfortable." Tell yourself that 100 times a day if necessary.
- Arrive early for any speech. Talk to others as they arrive. Test your presentation in chunks with them.
- Understand the expectations of the audience. Know your material. Present what you have in a way that meets their expectations while meeting yours too. In every way possible:

  (1) simplify, simplify, simplify;

  (2) make a point, then illustrate it with an example, story, or anecdote to bring it to life;

  (3) start and end with a thoroughly rehearsed 30 seconds.

- Illustrate points in various fashions: problem/solution, cause/ effect, general/specific (or vice-versa), simple/complex (or vice-versa), etc.
- Try to stay with *three* key areas. People can't seem to handle much more.

- Remember, even if it is complicated material, it can still be presented in an interesting way.

- Think back to the best and worst presentations you've ever seen and note what made them good or bad—then do the good, not the bad.

- Remember, you are "on stage" the minute you walk into the room, maybe even the minute you step out of your car in the parking lot. Act *on* long before you actually open your mouth and all the way until you exit.

- Eliminate useless words. In other words cut out jargon, buzz-words, fluff, and repetition.

- Let no filler words escape your lips (um, ah, okay, to be honest with you, you know, etc.). Just allow a little silence.

- Don't be defensive if people ask challenging questions. Smoothly throw it back to the audience if possible, and ask how they would address that.

- Practice your speech in your car driving to work: Shout it, whisper it, vary everything you can—volume, pace, inflection. Only by practicing in the extreme can you see what you're capable of sounding like and choose some variety to keep the audience's interest.

- Maintain a relaxed smile before, during, and after the presentation. It makes you look confident.

- To energize yourself just before talking, go outside to your car, or some such place to speak extra *loudly* for some practice, the way the football players do in their huddle. As you walk onto the stage or step behind the lectern, lower your shoulders, raise your chest, breath deeply, relax your jaw, and relax your feet.

- Start speaking.

- Debrief yourself after the presentation: What did you do well?

- What could you do better the next time? Save and review those notes before the next time.

Fall-back plans

- Motivate yourself with the thought that the most powerful communication there is is one human being standing up and speaking courageous truth. It may as well be you.

- Be audience-oriented, not self-conscious-oriented. Have as your goal the strong desire to have the audience *want* to listen. Get a little spiritual about your message.

- Write down verbatim every word you'd ideally like to say.

- Read it out loud at least three times.

- Now go back and really personalize it. Instead of using words like "the objective of the organization is . . .," write "my objective is . . ."

- Mark places to emphasize or deemphasize, gesture, and move your body.

- Add humor.

- Ask the audience questions to check for understanding, responsiveness, and receptivity. If you aren't getting those things, "immediately" is the time to do something about it.

- *Listen* to your audience; don't just talk at them.

- The day of the presentation, look for opportunities to customize comments to something happening in the news in that city, that day. You'll sound more relevant.

• Pump up the theatrics. Communication studies show words are
  only remembered 10 percent of the time. The rest—voice,
  physical presence, and the like—are remembered much longer.

NOTES

1. If that didn't work, I bolstered my chances by stopping and talking with some guy on the way
   to the restroom when my girlfriends weren't looking. That wasn't cheating; it was insurance,
   upgrading my chances and downgrading my friends'. That's the joy of competition, as long as
   you hold true to the spirit of the contest.

   P.S. one of the young men I met this way, Jim McBride, remains a friend to this day. We've kept
   track of each other's career and life, even though he lives in Moscow.

2. I recently talked with a telephone company representative on a customer service call. The
   woman said "let me see" 12 times in one phone call. In listening to messages I leave on people's voice mail, I've caught myself using the work "okay" too frequently. Sometimes it was a
   filler word, so I just eliminated it the next time I left the message. Now I use different words
   meaning the same thing: great, good, cool, that's right, etc.

USING EMOTIONAL ENERGY: IT'S WHAT'S BEHIND WHAT YOU'RE SAYING THAT SPEAKS LOUDEST

Emotional energy completes the picture of the well-coached individual. Throughout this book, I've written about your goal to be memorable, impressive, credible, genuine, trusted, and liked—on top of doing good work. Mental energy sets your course. Physical energy communicates it. Emotional energy gets others to concur. Usually before a colleague, peer, subordinate, or boss will concur with your goals, he or she asks these questions about you: (1) Do you know what you're doing? (2) Can I trust you? (3) Do you care about me? Everyone you deal with wants positive answers to all three.

Think about people you spend time with. My guess is you ask yourself the same questions about them. Do they know what they are doing? Do I trust them? Do they care about me? And when you ask if they care about you, you aren't expecting them to worry about you, have concern for you, take responsibility, make life easier, protect you, take care of you, or be nicey-nice. You simply expect their respect as a fellow human being: civility, courtesy, consideration. That is exactly what others want from you. It is not always easy to consistently give though, because people are such pains and they don't always deserve it. *Let's stop right there.* No one is at their best all of the time. Everyone is a pain in the neck at least some of the time. If this is how you feel, go back to Chapter 5 and attitude management. You'll first need to change your perspective about people.

MAINTAIN THE SELF-ESTEEM OF PEOPLE AROUND YOU

Your number-one job in life is to do all you can to maintain the self-esteem of people around you—while maintaining your own. That takes emotional energy. What do I mean by "maintain self-esteem?" It means to keep up, support, and believe in the person. Do it *always*, even when the person is not obviously deserving of it. Do not deliberately judge, attack, ignore, dismiss, criticize, or embarrass anyone. Start them out at 100 percent and let them take themselves down, if it happens that way. Do not start them at zero and force them to prove their worthiness to you.

There are a lot of good reasons to maintain others' self-esteem:

- Because that's the way you want to be treated.
- You understand what goes around comes around in life.
- It's practice to get better at your craft—good self-discipline.
- Who are we to judge? If we were wearing the same shoes as some person we have to deal with, we might do the same thing that person is doing.
- You are constantly being tested on how well you handle yourself in these situations.

The people who influence the decision on who gets the next assignment upwards are the ones you're trying to impress, and they make their decisions based on what they see. So by maintaining others' self-esteem, you are building your effectiveness and image as a manager. How, then, do you maintain yours and others' self-esteem?

1. Be clear, honest, open, and prompt to say what you will do and what you want others to do.

2. Accept any undesirable response or reaction for the time being.

3. Turn up the emotional energy effort.

A friend, Mindy Credi, is director of human resources at Pepsi-Cola in California. Part of her job is to lay people off. She makes a concerted effort to spend time in termination meetings telling people what they do well and what kind of company and situation would best benefit from their work. She doesn't just focus on what went wrong while at Pepsi. Even when they are headed out the door, she practices maintaining the self-esteem of others.

I once heard my agent, Mike Cohn, demonstrate perfectly this kind of self-esteem saving. He was talking to one of his new authors who had some spelling errors in her manuscript, "You're like President Kennedy, he couldn't spell either." It allowed the person to save face, while making a clear point about a developmental need.

Here's how another friend used it with me. I was working with a client, the vice president and general counsel of a telecommunications company, and used the word *mnemonic*. I mistakenly pronounced the first letter. My client knew the "m" was silent, so she said, "That's always been an interesting word to me, I'm going to look it up," as she reached for her dictionary. "Oh, the "m" is silent," she read, "I sometimes mispronounce it myself." Then she changed the subject. By handling that minor situation, she confirmed she was correct in her own usage for the future, minimized my embarrassment, and prevented my misuse of it in the future.

Now you could say, "I have a pretty good attitude, but I work with this jerk at the office and he never gives me any respect. Why should I give him any, much less maintain his self-esteem?" As hardworking, earnest, and effective as I try to be, I've been called a jerk at times. Perhaps you've been called one too. Am I one? Are you? Probably not. When you experience "getting" it, it makes you a little less likely to "give" it so readily. Dave Zodikof of Pepsi explains:

> The central issue for most people is not starting people out at 100 percent credit. It was for me. Changing my attitude about people has changed my life. It had a broader impact than just my career. At Pepsi I manage 35 people across four teams, formally mentor 10 people and informally a dozen more. Here's how I've helped others change their attitude too. At our first mentoring lunch, Phil and I talked for nearly an hour on his disappointment over being passed over for a promotion again. He'd been here nearly 10 years and had always excelled technically. His next promotion was to be a very senior technical position, where he needed the "buy in" from senior management, but he wasn't getting it.
>
> Being part of that senior management team, I knew Phil was seen as acting "superior" to everyone else, and of not sharing his technical information with his peers until he had fully analyzed it. I had seen this pattern before, and after Phil was finished telling me his full story, I walked him through the concept of starting people at 100 percent.

What this basically means is that you treat people as if they deserve 100 percent of the respect and trust that their position warrants. Phil was doing the same thing I had done in the past: Start people at 0 percent and make them work their way up. Phil made comments like, "She needs to earn my respect" and "He needs to prove to me that he's capable of handling this responsibility before I give it to him." Because he was starting people at 0 percent, they were constantly feeling that they had to prove themselves to him.

Trust me, people quickly get frustrated having to prove themselves to their bosses, much less proving themselves to every Tom, Dick, and Phil out there. Most people don't need or want to do this and they won't. The shift that Phil needed to make was to start people at 100 percent. Although this sounds easy, for many people it's a scary undertaking. Trust is not something people give easily, and it opens them up to be hurt.

The question that needed to be asked is if the risk is worth the reward. One important note is that the idea is to start people at 100 percent. That does not mean they stay at 100 percent. Some people work their way down pretty quickly, but some stay pretty high also.

I've seen the change before and it still amazes me. Literally weeks after Phil began starting people at 100 percent, changes occurred, in himself. He began to listen longer to what other people were saying and trusting them to draw their own conclusion from the facts. People began to be more at ease around him and include him in more discussions. Over the next few months Phil worked at starting people at 100 percent constantly, "fixing" his thoughts when they went astray. Eight months later Phil was promoted. Several people came up to me to comment on Phil's changes. They asked if I could help them too. I simply replied, "I'll tell you over lunch."

A high percentage of the time in life, we give people zero, you know, the ones you call morons, dweebs, nerds, imbeciles, and all the rest. They aren't really creeps and yo-yos at all. They're simply *shy* or somehow different from you and me. Lots of people are timid, reserved, introverted, apprehensive, guarded, and maybe even nervous. Therefore, it's more comfortable for them to focus on the technical side of things and ignore the people side. I know I've been timid, reserved, introverted, apprehensive, and guarded sometimes. I remember how uncomfortable it felt. I also remember if someone did or said something to support or help my belief in myself, I appreciated that person. It made me more tolerant of others who need to improve.

Once when I was shopping for hiking boots, the clerk was very helpful. I couldn't find a satisfactory pair, but the clerk kept bringing different options out until I was satisfied with my selection. While trying on the shoes, I made small talk with him. I found out he was newly married, just out of bible school, from Wyoming, and soon to become a pastor. I bought the boots. After trying the boots for a few days, I liked them so much I decided to buy a second pair. I called the store back and getting the store manager instead, I asked to talk to the clerk to see if he had an additional pair. I hadn't gotten his name, so I just described him, "Tall, sandy-haired, from Wyoming, newly married, going to be a pastor."

The manager said, "I have no idea who that would be." Now this is a store of less than 10 clerks, and the manager didn't know enough about her employees to identify the guy with the information I gave her! So the manager said, "Describe the boots. I know all the shoes." So I started with the brand name, and she chimed in, "Oh, that is model #4774. It's brown in color. We have one ladies size 9 medium left. In two weeks we'll be getting another shipment."

I fought the impulse to trash her as a poor boss, who knows her shoes but not her people. Instead, I tried, "I'll buy the extra pair, but I want to make sure that employee gets credit for the purchase. He was extremely helpful in finding the boots I liked. How can I make sure that happens?" She assured me she'd find out who it was.

Whether you are the manager or the one being managed, do everything you can to maintain the self-esteem of the people around you. If you're dealing with a human, he or she deserves it, just as you deserve it. Do not resent it when they don't give it back in the manner you want. (Maybe they haven't read the book!) Do it regardless, for *your* self-esteem. Managing and leadership is not rank, privilege, title, or money. It is responsibility—responsibility for helping people believe in themselves—maintaining their self-esteem.

BE THANKFUL FOR JERKS

Adversity is a true test of your ability. Difficulty is nothing but the best education you can get. Without problems, you don't know if you're really good or not. Problems only strengthen your mind, and sometimes your body. As the cliché goes, you don't learn to sail on smooth water. Besides, humans couldn't exist if everything unpleasant was eliminated. Think how boring it would be if no one ever got under your skin.

Joel Goldberg is a human resources executive accustomed to dealing with "difficult people" situations. In his earlier years he worked for a very competitive, outspoken, high-energy boss. The management team was at a team-building retreat. They were playing a form of the game *Jeopardy,* and the competitive boss got "ugly, heated, and out of control," says Joel. The boss was determined to win, even if it meant bending the rules.

The following morning, there was lots of grumbling from the

team, and Joel knew he needed to do something. While confirming the boss's competitive leadership as a valuable asset, Joel explained to the boss where he was guilty of team-defeating behavior. Joel also suggested how the boss might handle similar situations in the future when there was a need to stay in control and maintain the image of "leadership." He further proposed the boss serve breakfast to everyone involved. This little exercise in humility showed the guy's affable side and all turned out well. And Joel gained respect from both the boss and his colleagues because of how he dealt with this "politically charged" situation.

You learn from the difficult people—the least of which is *not to be one*. Despite how irritating they are, they do help to point out your areas of need. They keep you humble. And best, they make you strong. Coach John Madden used to tell his players, "When you get hit real hard, just laugh. The hitter thinks either you don't mind, or you like it, either way, it's good for the person being hit."

If you've been harassed by people, in a sense you've been chosen, and you have to ask yourself why. Something you're doing is inviting it. It's sort of like how a burglar selects a house as a target. He chooses the one he thinks he can successfully break into.

One of my clients called me to report on a situation. Her peer, a fellow director, had verbally pounced on her in front of her boss, accusing her of misguided management practices, which implied questionable character. He accused her of planting information with colleagues to undermine his directives.

With a modulated pace and controlling her voice volume, she addressed the possible confusion and clearly corrected his thinking by stating, "You can attack my approach, but I will not allow you to question my integrity in front of anyone, including our boss." She continued with an organized explanation of the circumstances and clearly explained what she wanted the colleague to do to correct the situation. I was proud of how she maintained her self-esteem while not lambasting his. Nevertheless, you don't maintain others' self-esteem at the cost of your own.

All in all, you can expect about six bad days a year brought on by jerks. Don't get obsessed by it or overly focused on it. It's part of your job. It's part of your paycheck. It's part of life. Accept that, "Okay, today is one of my six." Most people don't prepare for people and times that will really get them disappointed and discouraged, but both will eventually happen.

You prepare for the inevitable by:

1. Accepting that it will happen.

2. Deciding in advance you will handle it differently from how others would.

3. Trying to maintain the self-esteem of the people involved, yourself included.

Handling adversity adds tremendously to your book value. I'll explain.

YOUR BOOK VALUE

This sounds sort of crass but in most companies you are viewed on a *human asset accounting* basis, meaning your "book value" to the company. Bottom line, this means you're expected to contribute more to your organization than you cost it. Your book value varies throughout your career. You add to it with education, experience, accomplishments—often referred to as the "hard" side of business. You also add to your book value with executive maturity, presence, polish, and being memorable, impressive, credible, genuine, trusted, and liked—usually referred to as the "soft" side of business. Specifically, your book value increases when you:

CHAPTER SIX

- Decide to coach yourself
- Work on your style the way you work on your substance
- Eliminate fear in your life
- Are introspective about yourself and look for gaps to close
- Act the way you want people to view you

In the area of emotional energy, the three areas to work on are (1) being humorous, (2) being affable, (3) being bold.

BE HUMOROUS

Tune up your sense of humor. You're going to need it! Enjoy life. Give people around you a laugh. No, you don't have to start cataloging the latest jokes you've heard, but do try to *think* with a comic sense. "Laughter in the face of reality is probably the finest sound there is. In fact, a good time to laugh is any time you can." says columnist Linda Ellerbee.

Sometime back I was to give a speech at Howard University. The dean of the sponsoring department walked on stage to introduce me. "We looked all over the country to find someone to speak on professional presence. We couldn't find a black, so we found Debra Benton." People weren't sure whether to laugh or not, so we did. The easiest way to increase your effectiveness is through humor. If you can laugh, you can be effective. Laughter causes muscles to activate, then relax. People who suffer with arthritis, rheumatism, and other painful conditions get relief from the papin which is released in the body when they laugh. Laughter is how the oldest person in the world accounts for her longevity. (She lives in Arles, France, and is 121 years old.) If humor can help people who suffer real physical pain, it can help with the imaginary pain we too often feel in business. In fact, graduate business students at universities in Chicago, Nashville, and Denver are being taught stand-up comedy and improvisation to lighten up dry subjects. Among the benefits of humor are:

- It keeps you healthier.
- It enables you to share a common bond and draw a group together.
- It makes others around you feel good.
- It reduces stress in yourself and others.
- It gives balance.

The only criticism I've heard about humor in business is when it is sarcastic or caustic. Humor that is mean, nasty, or bizarre is usually ineffective in business.

Humor that is recognizable is best, the "I've been in that situation too," ironic type humor, like when President Reagan spoke at his alma mater, where he graduated with a C average. "Even now I wonder what I might have accomplished if I had studied harder," he quipped. Recognizable, right? And if you can't laugh at yourself, you'll just leave the job for someone else to do. Humor is a great *evener* of people and situations.

Professor Robert E. Provine spent six years studying giggles and guffaws. Among his findings:

1. People are around 30 times more likely to laugh in groups than alone.
2. The person who is talking chuckles 46 percent more than the people listening.
3. Four times more laughter is triggered by bland phrases than by formal jokes.
4. Women laugh more than men—except when listening to other women. Then, they generally clam up.

Provine found most laughter has nothing to do with jokes. In studying 1200 episodes of laughter, he found that only about one in five was linked to a deliberate effort at humor. "The big laugh getters? Dull stuff like, 'You've been doing what?' and 'Where have you been?'" Humor is the best way to maintain self-esteem and add to your book value. The ability to appreciate or express what is funny makes you affable.

BE AFFABLE

Emotional energy requires you to be pleasant and friendly, even when those around you aren't. Affability is more important than education, more important than credit and money. Being affable, mild mannered, and good natured is better even than quick wit. Affability is allowing for the failings in others, and that maintains self-esteem. The highest degree of niceness, according to Susan Lee, senior editor at *Forbes,* is "a gesture motivated solely by a sense of decency with no expectation of reward or recognition." And this from the *Baptist Trumpet,* "The character of a man can easily be judged by how he treats those who can do nothing for him." I remember watching a mentor of mine deal with a small business owner who was insignificant to his success. "Why do you do him such a big favor by going out of your way and giving him that information?" I asked. "He never does anything for you." He answered simply, "That's the kind of guy I am."

It's a big mistake, though, to try too hard to be liked. That is *not* what I'm talking about. I remember hearing about a CEO who wanted to have a reputation for being a good businessman and a good guy too. Someone told him he should walk around the plant more, chat with people, see how things were going. The only problem was, he walked around carrying a golf putter. When he'd stop and chat, he practiced a few strokes with an imaginary ball. In this case he didn't bond, he alienated. Mental, physical, and emotional energy must corroborate each other.

Affable doesn't mean trying to be approved of either. It does not mean being a weak leader. This lesson apparently got across to a client, who reported this unexpected finding: "My managing style is fairly laissez-faire. I let people do their own thing and try not to 'boss' them. The problem was my team was pretty ineffective. So I decided to do the opposite of what I typically do. Last Monday at the staff meeting, I directed who was going to do what, when. To my surprise, they responded cheerfully with, 'okay, boss.' We had the most productive week to date at this company."

Actually, I know I don't have to tell you to be "nice." You are or you wouldn't be where you are. I'll bet you're that way 95 percent of the time—with the people who open the door for you, let you have the taxi first, fill your coffee order just right, and so forth. It's that 5 percent of the time when some idiot causes you to be not-so-nice that I want you to work on. Don't succumb to the 5 percent who "get to you" like everybody else does. Do the opposite. Turn up your sense of humor. Go out of your way to get the results you want, but in an affable way! It will make you feel so satisfied.

Most important, being affable maintains self-esteem because you may be wrong about the person. They may not be a jerk. Remember, "walk a mile in their shoes." So if you aren't nice, you're the jerk! Don't even for 5 percent of the time be like the person I once heard described as, "He acts like he has no relatives." You're going to shake things up. People are going to be jealous. They aren't going to be agreeable or even cordial to you sometimes. But you can still choose to be amiable to them. Affable does not mean passive. Nice means nice—friendly, warm, refined. It does not mean being so congenial no one knows where you stand. Rather, you take a very definite stand, but deliver it in an affable way.

Affable wrath is expressed constructively:

- Keep cool most of the time so that when you get (theatrically) provoked, people know you really mean it.

- Have "wise rages" only, where it takes a lot to bring them out, and once out, they're over with quickly.

- Remember, anger gives power to inferiors, who become superior. When you suppress it, you save yourself a day or more of sorrow.

- It's popular to say count to 10 before acting when angered. Thomas Jefferson said count to 100. Thinking of consequences first sometimes prevents them.

A client told me the story of having an anger attack over work-related issues. During a business trip, she locked herself in her hotel room and for 24 hours solid watched the movie *Desperado*. She canceled business meetings and eventually she shook off the anger. She caused no damage to herself or others and in this way basically stayed in control during a crisis. As professional boxer Oscar de La Hoya says, "The key to success inside the ring is to stay in control." Cheerfulness and conviviality help you handle enemies smoothly.

No enemy is insignificant. One enemy for every fifty friends is still too much. You're probably wrong if you think you don't have any. When you see an animosity starting, try to reconcile or nullify your differences. (The up side of this is you have to be a "somebody" to have enemies.) Be realistic. There are selected times to not "make nice"—but not very often. I know life isn't always nice. Overcoming when it isn't makes it more so.

BE BOLD

Being humorous and affable does not exclude being fearless. Emotional energy requires confident, enterprising, even audacious attitudes and actions. What's neat is how these three areas work so well together. If you bungle some performance, your good-natured amiability gets you "forgiven" sooner. If you're liked and accepted by people, you get the support and confidence to do more courageous things. When you make bold moves, people admire you and like you. Remember attorney Lawrence Land, mentioned earlier? He wrote me about being "affably bold" when he went to the University of Miami.

> 20th Century Fox was previewing a first-run movie for free for two days (a sneak preview). Of course, this was a way for a great number of students to see the movie and spread the word. The name of this movie was "Hot Rock," starring Robert Redford and George Segal. The film producers and CEOs of 20th Century Fox were all there to promote the movie. After hearing the public relations people speak about the movie, I approached the producer to let him know that I was interested in public relations. He said that if you can think of an idea to help promote this movie, you are hired. Within three days, I thought of an idea and ended up getting hired. I also received two free cruises to Freeport and Nassau. The word got out very quickly that I was working for 20th Century Fox. I started receiving telephone calls from other PR people with Warner Brothers and Columbia pictures. Next, I promoted a movie for Cliff Robertson entitled J.W. Coop. Mr. Robertson asked me to consider working for him full-time. However, I had already been accepted to law school. Thinking back, I probably would have enjoyed working in public relations for the movie industry.

Bold acts build character and offer great opportunities as well. So sit down, calm down, throw up a little, and go do it. In the 1860s the Pony Express made communication possible from St. Joseph, Missouri, to Sacramento, California. Riders got paid $25 a week. A typical advertisement to get riders read, "Seeking young, skinny, wiry fellows not over 18. Must be willing to risk death daily. Orphans preferred." I'm not talking about that kind of bold. Nor am I suggesting you bungee-jump off the Washington Bridge or attempt to swim from Alcatraz to Pier 1 in San Francisco.

I want boldness to change your attitude when your upbringing taught you differently. Dare yourself to make the big bet 14 times a day. Catch yourself 100 times a day and correct missteps. Talk to strangers like you know them. Courageously walk into the next important meeting you have to attend and assert yourself in a manner that no one expects. (Make it effective, please. Pluckily wearing underwear on your head is not what I mean.)

Bravely, *act* more confident than you feel.

- You have to seek out the scary.

- You have to have the courage to go *against* your comfort zone.

- To knowingly choose courage is to save time.

- Remember: When the going gets tough, the tough get comfortable.

Be *unrealistic*. If you aren't unrealistic, you often set limits in terms of what you can do. With a dauntless resolve, maintain the self-esteem of people around you, even when they attempt to break down yours. Adventurously, test the use of some humor with the most straightlaced people you deal with. It's a personal challenge to me whenever someone says, "Whatever you do, don't joke with Mr. ___, he has no sense of humor. That becomes the first person I will kid around with. Those who dare to be bold risk a fall occasionally. An audience member asked about the percentage of time that being plucky and confident backfired. Less then 10 percent, I'd say. And again, your frame of mind and disposition keep you from succumbing to these setbacks. Never let up, even when you mess up, miss a step, or simply forget. Catch yourself 100 times a day.

Strategy consultant Joyce Scott used all the components of emotional energy in the following business situation.

In 1991 I was determined to break previous sales records in my new account. The only obstacles between my goal and reality were that I'd never gone to sales school, I'd never been a marketing representative, I'd never been responsible for a sales territory, and my new customer didn't want IBM trying to make sales calls. Other than those "opportunities," all was right in my world. My strategy, as the team leader, was to establish myself with some type of beachhead. My target was Raymond, who had experienced no help from our company, having been put into a terrible program.

As soon as I sat down in his office, he began to yell. He proceeded to yell, pace in front of me, move into my space, point dangerously close to my face, and sit back down for brief periods. He erupted for two solid hours to recharge. About 15 minutes into this routine I realized he was making some good points and I slowly opened my portfolio and began to take notes. I looked him straight in the eyes, listened to the words he said, ignored the cussing, and drew deep breaths every time he came near me. He ranted and raved, spit and spewed; I worked hard to keep myself glued to that chair.

When he finished, I said with an attitude of good cheer, in my slowest, strong but pleasant voice, "Raymond, are you finished?"

(continued)

He looked me straight in the eye and said yes. I stood up, walked to his desk, leaned over and said, "Don't ever let that happen again. I took you out of that program before I walked in here. I have a check for some of the damages. I've taken notes for you to compose a letter to IBM and work toward a resolution for the rest. Do you understand?" He nodded he did.

I finished explaining the plan of action and left his office. I felt my first exhale in two hours leave my body. I sweated completely through my suit. That meeting was a turning point that secured my place as the team leader. Raymond apparently left the meeting and told everyone, including the CEO, that I was a keeper and knew my business. I became one of IBM's top eight marketing representatives in North America and ended up attaining 233 percent of quota.

Emotional energy enables you to change, change every individual involved, and change destiny. Maintaining others' self-esteem is simple: clearly, honestly, openly, and early on, say what you will do and what you want others to do. Accept any undesirable responses or reactions for the time being. Turn up the emotional energy effort.

Questions to ask yourself

- Do I understand the importance of the emotional side of life in the professional world?

- Do I see how just being brilliant isn't sufficient?

- Do I want to control my effect on others versus leaving it to chance?

- Am I willing to take full responsibility for my effect on others?

- Do I see the potential for "leapfrog" growth in my personal and professional life if I focus on emotional energy?
- Do I appreciate the use of good humor from others? Can't I do the same thing myself?
- Am I a good-natured, affable person?
- Do I have the guts to do what it takes to be effective, regardless of how uncomfortable I might feel?

The answer should be "yes" to all the above.

Tools to fit the job at hand

- Maintain the self-esteem of people around you, both inside and outside of your professional life.
- Be thankful for jerks who teach you what you don't want to be, and help you grow into the person you do want to be.
- Check your book value today and recheck it every six months.
- Use humor as a leadership tool.
- Use affability as a leadership tool.
- Use boldness (of thought and action) as a leadership tool.

The variety of targets possible

- Don't fear MISTAKES.
- To better sell yourself and your ideas, think before you talk.
- Whatever it is you're afraid to do (but know has to be done), go ahead and just *do* it.
- Be an effective executive who has mental, physical, and emotional energy.
- Make a contribution in every meeting or gathering you attend.
- Hone an excellent sense of humor.

- Solve problems in an affable manner, as opposed to running over everyone in your way.

A Strategy to go forward: Handling Mistakes

- The good thing about mistakes is that no one will be jealous of you.

- If you try, you'll make mistakes. If you don't try, you'll really be making a mistake. (Besides, if you don't try, you miss the feeling of failure. And it feels so good to rise above failure.)

- Good leaders make mistakes; bad ones repeat them.

- Admit the mistake. Apologize if appropriate.

- Show no fear. Turn up the energy and even the theatrics.

- To prevent problems from reccurring,

  (1) Get timely, accurate information on what's going on *and* what went wrong, and fearlessly ask all the constituents involved;

  (2) Respond rapidly to what the information tells you and make changes where you can to correct the situation;

  (3) Above all, deal with the problem;

  (4) Relentlessly follow up, check up, and test to see how you're doing in correcting the mistake;

  (5) Don't let *that* mistake ever happen again.

- Most every mistake has a point at which you can turn it around if you are paying attention and willing to do something about it. To check for that point, follow the previous five steps *before* something serious occurs.

- The mistakes you can't afford to make (having read this book) are being invisible, arrogant, insensitive to others, solely money motivated, a bad role model, or phoney.

- The good thing about making a famous flop is that it will help keep you from becoming arrogant. Arrogance is what invites *really* big mistakes to be made.

- If you can't deal with failure, you can't win. For all their down side, the up side of errors is that they provide you information and opportunity for growth.

- Don't get me wrong; failure is not chic or cool. What you learn from setbacks is to not repeat them.

- If the mistake is that you lied, cheated, or stole, you have a bigger issue than can be addressed in this book.

Fall-back plans

- Panic, depression, overreaction, and hysteria are not fall-back plans. Mistakes will always happen. The difference is what you choose to do about them.

- The sooner you try, the sooner you'll make a mistake, and the sooner you'll get to the next level of learning, and the sooner you'll get ahead of the pack.

- Setbacks are only setbacks. Don't berate yourself. To help you get a better perspective, get feedback from people you admire about their mistakes and how they handled them.

- If you haven't made a mistake lately, fake one. Simulate a situation, an error, and what you "learn" from it. Do this before it actually happens so you don't have to have it happen, and you learn from it anyway.

- When a mistake is all over, go do some strenuous physical exercise to purge yourself of the negative energy.

- After you've showered and relaxed, write five things you've done well recently. You may want (or need) to remind your superior about those things to ease the memory of the mistake.

TEAM TIME: HOW TO COACH OTHERS

"Coaching just one person can change the lives of many people for the better: the benefits extend beyond the person to their family, friends, and unborn children. Additionally, the life of the coach is enriched by making a difference."

Lee Steuber of Pepsi-Cola, *a fellow coach*

A good way to coach yourself is to simultaneously coach others. I used the expression earlier in the book, "when one teaches, two learn." That is particularly accurate in the self-development areas we've been working on.

If you see someone else's "bad" attitudes, you'll likely try to not take them on also, because you see how destructive they are. When you hear people say negative things about themselves or their situation, it causes you to pay attention so you don't do the same. As you see opportunities for others to catch themselves 100 times a day, it will remind you of your own opportunities. When you see favorable situations for someone to "turn up" the theatrics to be more effective, you'll see them for yourself.

As you encourage, inspire, and motivate the person you're coaching to "stick to it," you just might yourself! You and the people you coach can grow more proficient in anything through intelligent observation combined with action. Although I coach people every day of my life, I also coach myself every day. For example, I was presenting the luncheon keynote speech at a national conference. Prior to my presentation, the group had another consultant speak to them on industry issues. He provided thoroughly valuable information but he spoke with such speed that it discounted him as an authority. I used the lesson to coach myself to *slow down*.

When my time came, I spoke in the most deliberate manner possible. I dramatically slowed down at times. I paced myself through my points as if everything I had to say was extremely important, therefore I was going to say it in an important way. Although I used a lot of energy, nothing was done in haste. Afterwards, the client said in a note, ". . .We had high expectations, but you exceeded them." Kudos feel good. Now, hopefully the content would have met their expectations anyway, but the purposeful delivery ensured that it did. The bottom-line benefit to you for coaching others: *You'll learn a lot yourself.*

IF YOU'RE GOING TO BE A COACH, BE A GOOD ONE

In *The Book of Five Rings,* the author, Miyamoto Musashi, writes, "Let the teacher be the needle, let the student be the thread, and practice unremittingly." To be a first-rate coach, you must set an outstanding example. People believe and trust what they see, not just what they hear. The better model you are for others, the easier it will be to coach them. To be a coach, you need to have something to offer. The best you can offer is to set an adequate standard. To be an "adequate" coach, practice everything we've been discussing. I'm not being arrogant when I say, that's all you need to do. One thing that will diminish your success as a coach is holding any information back like it is proprietary.

Native Alaskan fishermen have a name for greenhorns who come into their fishing grounds, *cheechakoes*. Some of them understandably harbor the attitude: "Why should we tell *cheechakoes* the things it has taken us years to learn the hard way? Why should we go out of our way to help them, then have them out in the fishing grounds competing with us?" That is an acceptable approach regarding native fishing grounds but unacceptable in coaching. An important element of coaching is getting information and resources into the hands of the person being coached. A book like this one is a perfect example. Once you've read it, share it.

TEN RULES FOR EFFECTIVE COACHING

If you think about it, you probably are a coach, official or unofficial, to someone already—a child, parent, co-worker, relative, or friend. That's good for them and you. When you help others get better, you'll likely get better yourself.

1. Cultivate the attitude that you do have something of value to offer someone. Do not be apologetic. You can be humble, but not recessive.
2. Be an impeccable example. For credibility's sake you can't, "Do as I say, not as I do."
3. Be other-oriented. You have to shelve your ego.
4. Slow down. It will make you look more self-assured (which breeds confidence in the coachee), and it will give you more time to think of good advice to offer.
5. Constantly raise the bar for yourself. As you get better experience, you'll be able to provide better advice.

6. Do not be intimidated by the coachee. She or he will likely be superior to you in some areas, but you are adequate and that it what you are offering.

7. Hold your ground. Some coachees will try to dismiss what you offer. If you have something of value, do not let them diminish it.

8. Do your job in giving superlative advice, but *do not* be bothered if the coachee doesn't apply it. Resenting the fact that he or she doesn't implement your thinking is naive. You teach. The person must want to learn.

9. Own up to your mistakes. If you gave advice that bombed, be willing to help extricate the coachee from any situation you helped get him into.

10. Stay objective. As much as you care for the coachee and her situation, you have to remain impartial. You will offer far better direction and be a much better coach if you can stay objective.

Steve Mangum is the CFO of Pier 1 Imports. He tells this story of coaching a person who was failing in the company:

> She came to the realization during the review process that she was not performing up to standard simply because her heart was not in her job. She liked it, but it didn't stir any passion or conviction, and therefore she had a lack of commitment to her work and it showed in her results. She was a lovely young woman who was probably one of the nicest people I have ever worked with. After the review, she left the company, went back to school, and got a degree in pharmacology. While there, she met her future husband. About a year after I had counseled her out of the company, she invited me to her wedding. At the wedding reception, she embraced me and told me that I had put her life back on track and that she was happier than she had been in years.

Be excruciatingly honest. If there is something you notice that needs to be said, have the courage to say it. Be smart, though, and say it in a way that won't shatter any egos or overly embarrass someone. (Remember to maintain their self-esteem.) But it is your responsibility to cover all the bases. Give the painful truth in the softest terms with an honest warmth, but on the other hand, do not go further than necessary.

I've known Sam Sanderson of Savvis Communications for some years. He's right up there in terms of competence, integrity, leadership, and all the rest that's required of someone at the top of an organization. I asked him how he'd describe what I do, "You spend time with people and nicely give pretty brutal feedback. In fact, you've mastered the art of brutal feedback. You tell people what they look like to the world. People have no perception how they are perceived, and you are their reality check." So give hard advice, and sweeten it with encouragement and praise.

Probably the most difficult of the 10 rules is number 8. The biggest frustration in giving advice is expecting people to take it. They don't always! Think back; you haven't taken all the good direction you've been given in life. So don't get disappointed if others don't take all of yours. Instead, get creative. Give it to them again, at another time, in a different and improved way. Try over and over, if necessary. Ask them how you can get through to them on something very important. Do what they say. Notice and acknowledge when they do follow good advice. And never say, "I told you so," despite the opportunities you'll have to say it.

Questions to ask yourself

- Do I have something of value to offer others?
- Am I willing to share instead of hoard information?

- Do I see how helping others can help me help myself as well?
  The answer should be "yes" to all the above.

Tools to fit the job at hand

- Set an impeccable example.
- Be other-oriented in the deepest sense.
- "Raise the bar" for yourself—*constantly.*
- Stand firm on your beliefs and direction.

The variety of targets possible
(issues your coachees will need help on)

- Dealing with office politics.
- Handling stress on the job.
- Inserting self in meetings.
- Dealing with boring, frustrating, time-consuming meetings.
- Managing procrastination.
- Managing time better.
- Corporate socializing.
- Getting and using a mentor.
- How to fire someone.
- How to handle being given too much work.

Strategy to go forward: Office Politics

- According to *USA Today* the greatest cause of stress at work is office politics, so you aren't alone in despising this plague.
- Take solace in the fact that as long as there are at least two people involved, there will be office politics.

- Spend the time it takes to worry about something by doing something about it.
- You must deal with office politics to minimize stress. Fortunately, it's not that difficult.
- First, be good at your job so attacks against your productivity are misguided.
- Deal with them early on and stick with it. One attempt to nullify attacks, innuendo, or mistruths isn't sufficient.
- Maintain your sense of humor. If you can't bring yourself to see the humor in the situation, you won't be effective in addressing the more difficult and uncomfortable ones.
- Be straightforward and direct when addressing others' infractions against you. If you fear calling them directly, you become part of the problem in office politics. To deal with a problem:

  (1) Research the validity of your concern;

  (2) If it is valid, contact the other person(s) involved and explain what you found;

  (3) Ask for their point of view;

  (4) If it is satisfactory, say so;

  (5) If it is not satisfactory, say so and tell the person you plan to discuss this with the boss;

  (6) Invite that person to be in on the meetings;

  (7) Explain to the boss the steps you've taken (1 through 6) and how you'd like things cleared up;

  (8) Get resolution and be sure everyone knows about it.

- Use humor and keep a good posture, a relaxed tone of voice, and a relaxed smile on your face during all of the conversations in the eight steps. Don't exaggerate or be sarcastic.

- Avoid judging the person's motivation; just deal with the reality.

- The next time another situation occurs, repeat the eight steps.

Fall-back plans

- Make notes, mental and otherwise, of details to use later if necessary.

- Treat people with a clean slate, despite their past history with you. You'd only want the same.

- Ask yourself, "Is there anything I can do in 5 minutes that will make this situation better?" Do that. You might avoid having to do all eight steps later.

- Don't burn bridges.

- The key to dealing with office politics is to not fear it. Address problems early. Be pleasant but firm. Offer alternative solutions. Say something pleasant to the parties involved when it is finished.

- It seems to take three encounters handled in this effective way before the other person clearly learns you cannot be toyed with.

- Politics runs rampant when there is a lack of control, lack of information, or lack of feedback. Don't let that happen to you.

- Again, remember, there isn't a person out there who doesn't have this same problem. How you handle the inevitable office politics will tell your boss more about your potential as a leader than just about anything you can do.

GOING ALL THE WAY: HOW TO HIRE A COACH

Take advice cautiously, but do secure it, and take it. If you decide you want an objective, professional, experienced person helping you, hire a coach. Don't rely on informal mentoring relationships. Most advice and direction given is too passive and is not focused on any method, whereas an effective coach will keep you on track, push you, and encourage and motivate you to be even better than you already are.

WHY HIRE A COACH?

I asked some of my clients why they originally sought coaching. Here are some of the reasons:

> *"I'm on the radar screen, and I really need your help."*
>
> *"To review strengths, needs, and opportunities."*
>
> *"For an objective sounding board."*
>
> *"To improve my performance."*
>
> *" I was getting somewhat bored and wanted to look at what some changes would mean in my life."*

"To answer the question for myself, 'Why am I in a big corporation and why am I not doing something different.'"

"For better clarity in opportunities, on what's outside."

"To help in my struggle to get off the merry-go-round."

"Gain personal control over my life. I don't want the corporation to rule my life."

"I needed it more than ever because of reaching a certain age."

"Quick-ups on my career."

"I had to accept the reality that I am really, really dispensable, and I didn't want anyone else to conclude that."

"I want to leave my stamp on people."

"I need to constantly raise the bar for myself."

"The more I value myself, the more others will value me."

"Who better to invest in than myself. Once I invest in myself, no one can take it away from me."

Whatever your reason, go all out in the personal effort. You'll likely only do this once in your lifetime, so do it to truly benefit you.

A WARNING AND A WARRANTY

The warning. Coaching is a very hot subject in business today. There is a proliferation of people calling themselves "career coaches." *The problem is all coaches are not created equal.* As in any profession, there are leaders, losers, and even lunatics. The fact is: There is a lot of commercial popularization and profiteering.

I happened onto an article that featured a 28-year-old office manager of an equipment supply company. Six months ago she read a news story about putting "spirit and soul" back into the workplace, something she felt was lacking in her own life. Instead of calling on a personal coach, *she became one!* A few months later, she is halfway through a "coaching university" program. She quit her supply company job and the next day conducted a "life-purpose" workshop. She reports having eight clients but wants thirty. This isn't just an isolated situation. I also recently heard of an insurance claims adjuster—of 19 years—who printed up a brochure offering his services as a coach. He could honestly use the slogan, "Serving clients since 9:00 A.M."

Now I am not questioning entrepreneurial spirit, drive, ambition, or the determination to start a business. Everyone deserves credit for effort. But people considering hiring a coach must really scrutinize what they are getting before they commit. I live in the middle of *Broncos* territory—the American Football League Champions in '74, '76, and '97. Every Sunday in every sports bar in town, there are thousands of "football experts" watching the game. They know all the rules and many of the tactics of both teams on the field. These fans are passionate about the Broncos' success. Despite their knowledge and "life purpose," not one of these people would qualify to take Mike Shanahan's job and coach John Elway!

You've probably heard the famous put down used for years about coaches, consultants, counselors, trainers and teachers in general: *If you can't do, teach.* In fact, many who can't do indeed teach. Many who can do can't teach. Any coach you consider should be able to do *and* teach, plus a whole lot more. "A whole lot more" is well illustrated in the old story in which a patient asks his doctor, "How can you justify charging $80,000 for an operation that only takes you one hour to do?" The doctor responds, "Because it took me 18 years to learn what to do and *what to do if something goes wrong* in that one-hour operation!" So my warning is to seriously consider who you allow to offer you advice. In other words don't take—much less pay for—advice from someone who needs it more than you do!

That reminds me of another old joke. Two bums on skid row were discussing how they ended up there. One said, "I'm here because I never listened to anyone's advice." The other said, "I'm here because I listened to everyone's advice." Truth is, there can be a lot of money made in the coaching and business consulting world. Experienced ones charge from $2500 to $10,000 a day. (The woman mentioned above charges $50 a session, so at least her clients aren't risking much.) Money is a magnet causing a lot of unhappy or unemployed people to hang out their shingles as "coaches."

What too many clients are paying for is *inexperienced* advice that may get them into more trouble than they could get into by themselves. And what's worse for the profession, every dissatisfied client will tell on average 250 contacts about how rotten business coaches are.[1] That gives qualified professionals a black eye through association.

If I sound a bit harsh on some "coaches," it's because I care so much about the recipients of the advice. A coach is totally useless unless she or he immeasurably increases an individual's performance, both personal and professional. It isn't sufficient to know how to "play the game." That helps, but coaching is its own discipline. I'd much rather you coach yourself than allow an unqualified person to do it. That's why I wrote this book: to show you the rules, tactics, and what to do when something goes wrong in your professional life.

Sometimes you have to hire a coach yourself; sometimes your company will hire one for you. When I list clients like Pepsi, Motorola, Allied Signal, Nabisco, Colgate, Frito-Lay, etc., those are companies hiring me to work with their managers and executives. When a company sends an individual to me, I clearly explain to the client and the individual I'm coaching, "The company is paying my fee but you are the client. You are the one I'm concerned with. I'm not here to make you into something your company wants. I'm here to help you be the best you can be, wherever and whatever you are doing."

Likewise, this book provides you, the reader, my client, with:

1. "Inside info" that goes on in expensive coaching sessions.

2. Specific coaching tools and strategies to help you go out and compete with the heavy-hitters on an equal playing field.

3. Advice to keep you out of the hands of charlatans who'll waste your money and worse, your time and energy.

The Warranty. If you utilize my advice, I can guarantee that your performance will increase. If it doesn't, I'll personally give you your money back on this book. You can write to me and tell me why it did or didn't work for you. The address is: Benton Management Resources, 2221 West Lake Street, Fort Collins, Colorado, 80521. My e-mail: debra@bentonmanagement.com

Also, if you write and tell me your success stories, they might find their way into my next book!

HOW TO FIND A COACH

Ask people you respect if they have used a coach or know of one they'd recommend. Try to narrow it down to three choices to interview. Don't worry where the coaches are located geographically. Their information and resourcefulness is more important than their addresses. In asking people for a resource recommendation, also ask what the person is best at and where the person helped the most and the least. You want to make sure their "best" is what you need and that their worst is insignificant to you.

Don't assume your coach has to come from your industry. An insurance salesperson friend thought he had to go to an insurance coach. The up side of that is that there will be a common language between them. The down side is that the "specialist" coach may lack cross-disciplinary knowledge. You want a coach who knows enough about your industry to relate to your situation, but who knows a lot about other industries as well. Sometimes, people who criticize a coach didn't utilize the coach well or didn't want to follow the advice, so that doesn't necessarily mean the coach lacked ability. But sometimes the coach does lack experience and ability in an area. The key is to find that out in advance. No one coach will be able to solve every conceivable problem, but she sure should be able to deal with a majority of them.

Be aware that of the people who can effectively coach you, not all call themselves coaches. They might be called business advisors or management, business, or career consultants. As a last resort, consult a directory of coaches. But remember, since there is no checking of qualifications, good ones will be there alongside not-so-good ones. Unless you know someone using them, it is hard to read and evaluate from the directory.

When you've narrowed your list to three, contact their offices and request information. Read the information. Telephone and talk to the coach you are interested in. Don't allow them to put you through to a salesperson selling the firms' services. You must talk to the coach personally. If they don't have time to talk to you now, they definitely won't later. Too often, a smooth-talking salesperson is your contact. They will select and assign the coach best suited for *their* purposes. What that can mean is that they'll assign you to the one who needs the business the most.

Insist on talking to the person you would be working with. Ask the person:

- What can I expect to achieve working with you? (The answer should be something you want to achieve.)

- How do we take advantage of what I already do well? (The coach should be asking you some questions to learn what you do well, your strengths and weaknesses.)

- What mistakes will you help me avoid? (The coach needs to be helpful when things go wrong.)

- Would anyone be working with me besides you? (Ideally, no one else would be. You don't want to get a second- or third-tier person assigned to you.)

- How would we work together? (It varies. Just make sure it is a manner and timetable you are comfortable with.)

- What will I get from you? (What you get should include both what you know you need and what you don't know you need.)

- Why are you in this business? (The answer should be because they have a burning passion to provide this kind of service. If it is just a job for them, they might go get another job in the middle of your program.)

- Why should I elect to work with you? (Let the person show how she sells herself. Since this person will be teaching you, make sure you like what you hear.)

- When would we be able to start? (It should be within a reasonable timeframe that meets your needs and the coach's schedule.)

- How is your schedule/volume? Would I have the time I need with you? (You need to feel comfortable that you won't get lost in the volume.)

- How long do we work together? (This varies based on the program you pick.)

- How do you charge for your services? (Generally speaking, coaches who charge more are worth it or they couldn't charge that much. This isn't always true, of course. Some just have the guts to charge a lot but offer marginal service. An experienced coach charges $2500 to $10,000 a program.)

- Do you have a track record of helping individuals accomplish their goals? (If you want to, ask to talk to some of the coach's clients as references.)

When you ask the questions, listen to the answers analytically, but listen with your heart also. Who *feels* right for you. Trust your judgment and go with that person. You should conclude the person is experienced, knowledgeable, relevant, practical, thought-provoking, encouraging, inspiring, stimulating, genuinely concerned in helping others, respectful of you, dynamic, fun, refreshing, enjoyable, credible, honest, trustworthy, sincere, and down to earth.

You want a coach who has worked with many business professionals and who has been involved in numerous business challenges at all levels of the organization. When the comfort level is there, start keeping a trigger log of issues and situations you want to discuss with your coach.

Here's a checklist to use when evaluating your coach *and* when using a coach, so you both stay on track:

Thorough in approach.	_____
Creative in offering a solution.	_____
Redefines your view of the situation.	_____
Diagnoses the cause of the problem.	_____
Is accessible.	_____
Keeps commitments.	_____
Doesn't waste time.	_____

Listens well. _____

Speaks free of jargon. _____

Relates well to people. _____

Lets you know in advance what you'll be doing. _____

Keeps informed on progress. _____

Has a good understanding of your business. _____

Makes you more effective at what you do. _____

You want a coach who helps you do things you didn't think you were capable of. You want someone who is your champion, confidante, watchdog, thought-partner, sounding-board, personal trainer, and focus puller.[2] You want someone who will help you become even more of a contender, not a pretender. You need a coach who's won and lost, who knows both sides, and knows how to prepare you. Buffalo Bill Cody described himself as, "seventy-two—and two hundred years in experience." You don't want someone 72, but the 200 years experience is possible, *figuratively* speaking.

Here are three final key points to take away:

1. Be careful who you select to coach you.

2. Make them work for you and earn their money.

3. Listen and act on their advice *before* you feel you're ready, because you probably are.

NOTES

1. The funeral industry estimates the average attendance at a person's funeral to be about 250, hence my use of that figure to indicate the number of people one might tell about a bad coaching experience.

2. This list comes directly from my clients, when I asked them to describe an effective coach. One called me her "mental spa day."

Your Own Personal Playbook

1. Everybody needs coaching.
2. You can coach yourself.
3. You have to start this instant.
4. Substance isn't sufficient; you need an effective style too.
5. It's never too late.
6. Eliminate (or hide) your fear—and get going!
7. Take the time necessary to review yourself and gather others' perceptions of you.
8. Isolate your trigger situations.
9. Set goals to handle those situations.
10. Your mind is the foundation for everything.
11. You are adequate.
12. Do the opposite.
13. People believe what they see, so give them a good show.
14. You are totally in control of what they see, so give them a good show.
15. Tenaciously, slow down and act up.
16. Be humorous.
17. Be affable.
18. Be bold.
19. Maintain the self-esteem of people around you.
20. Set an impeccable example.
21. Give them what you wish others would have given you.
22. Do this for the people you love . . . and who love you.

INDEX

ABOUT THE AUTHOR

D. A. Benton is president of the research and consulting firm Benton Management Resources, Inc. With an international client list that ranges from the Fortune 500 to political candidates, she is renowned for her ability to improve the performance levels of executives, and by extension their organizations. She writes for numerous magazines and newspapers, including *The Wall Street Journal,* and has been featured in numerous publications and broadcast outlets, including *Time, BusinessWeek, Fortune, The New York Times, USA Today,* "CNN," "Good Morning America," "CBS Morning News," and "The Today Show." She is the author of three books, including the bestseller *How to Think Like a CEO.*